I0553438

PRAISE FOR
SLIPPERY OCHRO

"A trip down memory lane…a delightful look into the rustic country life in Guyana in the 1960s and 1970s…something for everyone, and the scheming, the simple innocence, the rum shop culture, the sexual innuendoes, the greed, and the wise counsel of the village fathers, make for enjoyable reading. Kennard has a gift of bringing his characters to life as the story unravels."

—Carl B. L. Morgan, Colonel (Ret)—

"In this delightful, fast moving and often humorous tale, Guyanese Canadian writer Ken Ramphal transports us to the nostalgic village of Canal Number 2 Polder. We are swept along by the exploits of the village huckster and confidence trickster, aptly nicknamed Slippery Ochro, and his wife, Phulmattie."

—Ram Jagessar—
Author: *The Man Who Broke the Lottery*

"Ramphal's gripping tale is based on two real-life characters, but we all know people like Slippery Ochro and Phulmattie. Ramphal's work is universal. A must read."

Roop Misir, Ph.D.
Author: *OAC Biology Workbook-Student's Edition*

i

ALSO BY KENNARD RAMPHAL

Seeram's Illusions
Teacher Ram's Fascination With Fire
Dilchand Joins The Army
Escape To The Canadian Jungle

Co-Author with Barbara Verasami and Dwarka Ramphal
Imprints In Life's Journey

SLIPPERY OCHRO
A Novel
3rd Prize Guyana Prize For Literature
Fiction: 2023

Kennard Ramphal

MiddleRoad | Publishers

www.middleroadpublishers.ca

Making Literature See The Light Of Day

Copyright ©

2nd Edition published by

www.middleroadpublishers.ca

2024 Kennard Ramphal and MiddleRoad Publishers

Library and Archives Canada Cataloguing in Publication

Ramphal, Kennard, author

Editor Ken Puddicombe

ISBN 978-1-990765-37-7 (soft cover)

Front Cover design by kathryn.lagerquist@gmail.com

Back cover layout by Ken Puddicombe

www.kenpud.wordpress.com

"Give them an inch and they'll take a mile, states an English proverb, and so goes the story of Mohabir and Dularie when they allow Slippery Ochro and his wife, Phulmattie, to build a small house on their property. The setting is the rustic village of Canal No. 2 Polder in British Guyana, prior to the country's independence in 1966. The residents earn their living from farming and working on the Wales Sugar Estate. and lead simple lives in traditional fashion. The characters speak in their local English dialect, which is skillfully used to develop the plot as the timeless story unfolds."

—Elaine Balpataky, Retired teacher/librarian—

DEDICATED

This book is dedicated to my parents and the residents of Canal No. 2 Polder, Demerara, Guyana, who raised me. "It takes a village to raise a child."

Table of Contents

ACKNOWLEDGMENTS

My eternal gratitude to my wife, Orna, who patiently endured my being a ghost in the house during periods of intense writing, and who read many drafts of the novel. Many thanks to my children, Savita, Yogita and Rejendra, and my sons-in-law Max Naraine and Simon Eberlie, for their constant encouragement.

My sister Barbara Versami and my brother Dwarka Ramphal read and commented on the many drafts, and the novel is better for it.

As always, the members of the CARICAN group of writers, Ram Jagessar, Roop Misir and Harry Persaud, were there to offer constructive criticism, advice, and on occasion, prodding.

Thanks to Ken Puddicombe and MiddleRoad Publishers for editing, proof-reading and publishing this 2nd Edition.

Chapter 1

"All mankind is divided into three classes: those that are immovable, those that are movable, and those that move."
—Benjamin Franklin—

Everybody in Canal No. 2 Polder was so afraid of Slippery Ochro and his wife, Phulmattie, that most of them endeavored to become friends with the couple. Experience had taught them that the two were known to bring vengeance down on those who were responsible for any real or perceived insult or rejection. They also were well aware that if Slippery Ochro and Phulmattie were not their friends, they would eventually become their enemies. Only the very naïve or foolhardy would want to be enemies with the couple, who had hounds' noses for conflicts and court cases, and were certain to be involved on one side or another in a disagreement.

Slippery Ochro's real name was Sugrim Singh, but because he was so smooth and devious, people called him *Slippery Ochro*. In time, people forgot his real name, and everybody, including his wife, called him "Slippery Ochro." A thin dark man, with a cunning smile, he considered joining the estate truck every morning to go and work in Wales Sugar Estate, beneath him. He did not own or rent any land to plant a farm, or build a house, but he and Phulmattie lived in several small, thatched houses he and his cohorts built with local materials. The couple moved frequently, because invariably, Slippery Ochro and Phulmattie had disagreements with the owners of the land on which their hut was built, and they would then manage to convince another landowner to allow them to build a hut on a corner of his land.

Phulmattie, a thin, dark woman, had her teeth in the upper and lower jaws covered with gold caps, fitted by the quack dentist, Baleigh, who rode through the village every Thursday on his motorcycle. Most people had wives or husbands who acted as foils to each other. If, for instance, the man is a spendthrift, his wife would attempt to curb his spending. On the other hand, if the wife has a tendency to meddle in other people's affairs, the man would try to rein in his wife's inquisitiveness. It would be an understatement to say that Phulmattie, wasn't a foil to Slippery Ochro's penchant for court cases. In fact, many people argued that Phulmattie relished court cases more than Slippery Ochro, as she flitted from house to house in her multi-colored *rumal*,[1] flashing her famous gold-toothed smile, as she gossiped with fellow villagers with easy familiarity.

**

Mohabir and his wife, Dularie lived in a fairly large house with a front verandah which ran along the entire width of the house. They owned a piece of land with a wide frontage. The house was built on the eastern boundary of the land, and the large tract of land on the western side was covered with coffee and fruit trees. The couple was so well respected in the village because of the size of the land they owned, but more importantly, because of their upright lifestyle, that people called Mohabir *Sadar*, meaning one who is a leader in terms of an upright lifestyle.

One sunny afternoon, at about 2:00, Mohabir was dozing in the hammock in the living room when a loud knocking on the front door startled him. He groggily went to the door to answer it, and was surprised to see Slippery Ochro on the landing. Slippery Ochro, was dressed in black trousers, and a checkered red and white shirt. He wore a straw hat and a cunning smile. Like most people in Canal, he was barefoot.

"Sadar, I sorry to disturb you, but I come to ask you a small favor. People all over Canal say how you kind, and I know you won't refuse me."

"We in Canal always help one another," Mohabir replied, expecting Slippery Ochro to ask him for some fruits, or a small amount of money.

"Singh say that he gon sell his house and land. He ask me to move me house. I know that you got plenty land. Can you kindly allow me and Phulmattie to build a small hut on a corner of your land?" Slippery pointed to the west of Mohabir's property. "There gon be many coffee, mango and other fruit tree between our house, so we na gon see each other. We na gon bother you."

Mohabir looked at Slippery Ochro and thought, *I do not want this man and his wife to be my neighbors, but I don't want to be his enemy either. Me and Dularie living nice and peaceful. What excuse can I make?*

---

[1] Cloth headdress

- 2 -

"Nobody can trouble you if I build a small house on your land," Slippery Ochro added, as an incentive. "Me and Phulmattie gon look after you and Dularie."

"I got to ask Dularie about it," Mohabir finally said.

Slippery Ochro, lived up to his reputation of being a quick thinker, and immediately retorted, "You right! We gon to get the women involved in these things. I gon[2] ask Phulmattie to come and speak with Dularie."

Mohabir was mesmerized, and could only stare at Slippery Ochro with a blank look on his face.

Slippery Ochro broke the awkward silence. "After Phulmattie talk with Dularie, I gon come back tomorrow afternoon. Thank you, Sadar!"

As Slippery Ochro walked down the stairs, Mohabir stared at him, and wondered what had just happened.

Mohabir knew he was in a quandary, and deciding to seek his wife's advice, went into the kitchen, where he saw Dularie at the sink. Looking at his wife, with her waist length hair, her beautifully embroidered white *rumal* and her slim figure, despite the fact that she was fifty-four years old, Mohabir thanked the gods who led him to a good wife. It had been thirty-eight years since they were married in a *bamboo wedding*[3] and Mohabir enjoyed every single day of those years. He enjoyed Dularie's smile every morning when he walked in the kitchen where she would already have coffee, roti and some fried vegetables ready. He enjoyed eating every meal she cooked. He enjoyed making love to her in the nights. But when he reflected long enough, the quality he appreciated most of all was her unwavering loyalty to him, especially when things were not going his way.

He remembered when he lost his job in the estate office, and he came home depressed...

**

"They tell me that they don't have space for me at the office, and that if I want to work in the estate, I got to go and work in the field," he had told Dularie.

Dularie had put her hand on his shoulder and earnestly reassured him. "With all your education, they want you to work in the field? They want you to cut cane? We got some savings and enough land to grow coffee and

---

[2] Short form of "going to"
[3] Wedding in a Hindu ceremony, not considered legal at that time

fruit trees. We can live with the little money we save, and we gon make more selling provisions and fruits. And you can go to work when you want to, and stay home when you want to. And no *bakra*[4] man can tell you anything."

**

Mohabir was unsure of how to introduce Slippery Ochro's request, and asked Dularie as a way of greeting, "What you doing?"

"I just *mangaying some bartan*.[5] Come sit down and let me take out your food."

"Before you take out my food, I want to tell you something. Can you leave the bartan and come and sit with me for a while?"

When Dularie saw her husband, brows furrowed, and scratching his head vigorously, she knew that it was something important. Whenever Mohabir was worried, he scratched his head, sometimes until there was blood under his fingernails. She immediately wiped her hands on her apron and sat at the table. She did not like to see her husband, who generally had a cheerful demeanor, and who always liked to tell jokes and anecdotes, worried like this, and wondered what happened recently to upset him. They had a good coffee crop, their provision farm was thriving, and their fruit trees were providing enough fruit which they sold every week to Kandhai, who took it to Stabroek Market to sell to the people in and around Georgetown.

"Slippery Ochro come to see me, and he just left," he told her.

"Yes, I see you and he talking. I know that you know him, and I know that you na gon[6] get involved with him or his wife. Both of them get involved with *other people's story*,[7] and both of them *walk with their mouth*,[8] and like to take people to court. What he want?"

Mohabir hesitated, and scratched his head. "He ask if he can build a small house on our property. He got to move, because Singh selling his house and land. He say that there gon be many trees between the two houses. I did not know what to say, so I tell him that I gon talk to you. He

[4] White man
[5] Washing dishes
[6] Short form for "not going to"
[7] Other people's business
[8] Gossip

say that Phulmattie gon come and speak with you this evening." Mohabir breathed a sigh of relief at being able to get it all out.

"Oh Bhagwan! What worries you bringing pon me head!" Dularie looked at the ceiling and pressed her right hand to her forehead.

"I don't want them people living near us," Mohabir said, as he scratched his head furiously. "They are trouble with a capital T. But what you gon tell Phulmattie when she come?"

Dularie needed some time to think, so she rose from the table, walked to the fireside, and re-arranged the wood before she returned and sat opposite her husband. Her mind was working overtime as she tried to decide how she and Mohabir could get out of this situation.

When she returned to the table, she said, "I know how they spiteful. They can turn everybody against us, and people gon think that we wrong. Look when Noor had problems with Ishmael. Slippery Ochro and Phulmattie went to Ishmael first, and Ishmael want nothing to do with him. Then they go to Noor and side with Noor. And they get the whole village bad-mouthing Ishmael and saying what a thieving, evil man he was. I don't want them to do the same thing with us. People know them , but still allow themselves to be fooled by them. How they do it?"

Mohabir had calmed himself down by this time. "They smooth. They start by making friends with you, and then they start telling you little things. Once they got you hooked, they get you involved in bigger things. But we talking about what you gon tell Phulmattie when she come this evening."

"I don't know what to tell her. I don't want them living near me, but I don't want them to start telling stories about us, and make people hate us."

"You think people gon like us if we let Slippery Ochro and Phulmattie live on our land near us?"

Mohabir and Dularie looked at each other for a long time, each trying to think of how to solve the quandary with which they were faced. They were interrupted by a knock on the door, and when Dularie opened it, she was face to face with Phulmattie, her gold teeth flashing in the light. She was about the same height as Dularie, and wore a blue flowered dress, with her hair done up in a bun. Her eyes darted from Dularie to her house and to the surrounding property, as if assessing her new living environment. Dularie did not know why she was intimidated by Phulmattie's presence.

"Heh, eh gal, how you do?" Phulmattie said.

Dularie caught the strong odor of garlic on Phulmattie's breath and after a long pause, felt obliged to reply. "Fine! How you doing?"

- 5 -

This was the break Phulmattie wanted.

"Oh, so, so gal! Singh gon sell his land to Maraj, and Maraj want we to move before he buy Singh house and land so that he can build a *matyia*.[9] Maraj pretend to read *Ramayan*[10] and pray, but his wife mouth a run like river. And he ah watch them young gal like he want bore through them with his eyes, but he want us to move our house so that he can build a matyia. Dularie gal, we na gon trouble nobody. We gon build a small house so that rain wouldn't wet us, and sun won't burn us, and we got somewhere we can put we head down at night. God gon bless you. Some people keep they place so nasty that you scorn to drink a glass water in their house, but we gon keep the place so clean that you can eat off the floor."

Dularie was dumbfounded, and when her husband joined her at the door, she didn't know what to tell him.

Phulmattie spoke for here. "Heh, heh, Mohabir, you belly getting big. Like you becoming rich! I just telling Dularie that we won't bother nobody. Not everybody in this village kind like you two. Most people won't give you a banana to save yuh life. But I been telling Slippery Ochro how you two so kind that you would give people the clothes off your back. We gon build a small house with a *juk grass*[11] roof, and we won't bother anybody. And we wouldn't let anybody bother you either. You know that we be quiet people, but we don't take *rass pass*[12] from anybody. And we don't let anybody take they eyes pass we friends too."

It was the last sentence that prompted Mohabir and Dularie to look at each other and nod in an implicit agreement to let Slippery Ochro and Phulmattie build their house on their land. They knew that they were getting old, and that many of the younger boys in the village would not show them the respect that the older people who knew them better would show. *It would be nice to have somebody to represent us in our old age*, they both thought.

"Okay!" Mohabir told Phulmattie. "Tell Slippery Ochro that you can build a small house between the star-apple and the mango tree. Build it about three hundred yards from the drain. And you can pick fruit from the trees to eat, but not to sell."

---

[9] Hindu temple
[10] Hindu holy scriptures
[11] Grass used for thatching
[12] Abuse

"I gon tell Slippery Ochro that you agree. The two of you so nice and soft. We won't let anybody take advantage of your kindness. We gon start building this week-end."

Phulmattie's gold teeth flashed triumphantly as she turned to go home, leaving Mohabir and Dularie vacantly looking at each other. Like zombies, they returned to the kitchen and sat down. They were fully aware that they couldn't blame the other for what they realized was a foolish decision. And both knew that it would be even more foolish to go back on that decision.

Finally, Mohabir broke the silence. "We couldn'a do anything else."

"She know that we have the land. And she know that we soft and like to help people. Remember that people help us too, when we just got married. If we tell she, *No*, they gon tell everybody in Canal that we got the land, and we didn't allow them to build they house on we land."

"But we didn't take advantage of the people who help us. You think that Slippery Ochro and Phulmattie gon take advantage of us because we soft?" Mohabir asked his wife, already knowing the answer.

Dularie endeavored to reassure her husband. "We got to make sure that he can't take advantage of us."

In this manner, the couple consoled themselves and each other as they went about preparing their dinner. But deep down they acknowledged that they were out-maneuvered, and harbored resentment towards each other for allowing Slippery Ochro and Phulmattie to outsmart, intimidate, and manipulate them. Over dinner, Mohabir and Dularie looked at each other, and then turned away many times in an uncomfortable silence. After they had finished eating, Mohabir did not help Dularie take the dishes to the sink as he usually did, but went to the verandah to smoke his pipe.

It our house and land, he thought. *How did we let Slippery Ochro and his wife outsmart us? We know who they are, and still we let them pull one over us. Once they start building their house on our land, we can't stop them. Dularie should not let Phulmattie smart her out like that.*

However, as Mohabir continued smoking, and thinking about the situation, he conceded, *Why I blaming Dularie? I should have said 'No.' Why didn't I say 'No?' Is it because I am too kind, or am I scared of Slippery Ochro? So many people take advantage of me because I can't say, 'No' to them. What wrong with me? Dularie is the same. She too soft to refuse people anything. Thank God that we got this big piece of land and that we live off the money we get for coffee, and fruits and vegetables.*

Mohabir finished smoking the tobacco in his pipe. As he dusted the pipe into the ash tray on the ledge of the veranda, he made a resolution. *Let Slippery Ochro and his wife build their house on the piece of land that we agree on. But that will be all. I gon have no more business with him.*

The stars were already dotting the sky, and Mohabir heard an owl hooting when he got up from the verandah and went into the bedroom where Dularie was already in bed, lying on her side with her face away. He changed into his pajamas, knowing that she did not like the smell of tobacco on his clothes, went under the sheet, and snuggled up to her.

Dularie was awake, but did not say anything because she knew that her husband was upset. She was also upset with herself for letting Phulmattie manipulate her, but was more concerned about Mohabir's reaction to what was happening. She was prepared for a period of relative silence from him, during which he would figure things out, and come to some sort of resolution. When he spooned her, she smiled, knowing that all would be well.

"Let Slippery Ochro and Phulmattie build a house and live. But that is all. We gon have no further business with them," Mohabir consoled his wife.

Dularie said nothing, but acknowledged Mohabir by moving closer to him. They both fell asleep, still disturbed, but content that they were not angry with each other.

**

Slippery Ochro and Phulmattie visited them again the following day, and they went with Mohabir to pinpoint the exact spot on which the house would be built. After the decision was made, there was no stopping the new non-paying tenants. The weather co-operated the following Saturday, and Slippery Ochro and some of his cronies took advantage of the warm sunny weather, and cleared the land of the few trees and shrubs on it. When Mohabir went to see how things were progressing, he frowned when he saw his star apple tree on the ground, but remembered that he had another star-apple tree behind his latrine.

Slippery Ochro saw Mohabir, dropped his cutlass, and approached him. "We just clearing the place up. "Tomorrow, we gon cut *manicole*[13] to

---

[13] A thin palm tree, which can be split and used to build the walls and floors of houses

do the wall and floor. After that, we gon put on the roof, and then we can move in and take we time doing the rest."

Mohabir was astonished by the speed at which the house was being constructed, but all he could do was nod his head, as he glanced ruefully at the star-apple tree. "Where Phulmattie?" he asked Slippery Ochro, because he felt that he was expected to say something.

"Oh! She gone with Sumintra and Elsie to cut long grass to thatch the roof," Slippery Ochro replied. "You don't have coffee drying in front of your house," he observed, referring to the clear space in front of Mohabir's house, which he used to dry his coffee before taking it to Baba, who had a mill to separate the coffee beans from the dried pulp. "I gon put the long grass there to dry for a few days before we do the roof."

Mohabir felt that there was little he could say, and nodded his assent, before returning to his home and Dularie.

As they were relaxing after dinner on their verandah later in the evening, they saw Phulmattie and her two helpers fetching bundles of long grass, which they deposited in front of their house. They all wore straw hats, and their long skirts were hitched on their waists.

Phulmattie dropped her bundle of grass, wiped the sweat from her face, and looked at Mohabir and Dularie. "We gon just spread the long grass here to dry for a few days, gal. Then Slippery Ochro gon get dem boys to do the roof." She directed her gaze to Mohabir, flashed her gold teeth at him. "I tell dem girls how kind both of you are. You allow us to build our house on yuh land. We got more bundles to bring," as she and her helpers left to fetch more roofing materials, leaving Mohabir and Dularie to wonder at the swift progression of activities.

Both Mohabir and Dularie refrained from visiting the site on Sunday, because they knew that they would be upset at the rapidity at which Slippery Ochro and Phulmattie were encroaching in their lives. However, they were aware of the flurry of activity on the part of Slippery Ochro and his friends at the building site. When Mohabir strolled over just before dinner on Monday afternoon to see how things were progressing, he was astonished. Slippery Ochro, shirtless and a scarf tied around his head, was working with three of his friends, who were also shirtless. They had already planted the posts, which were simply the trunks of trees cut from the forest on the other side of the conservancy, and had finished nailing the *manicole* strips to form the walls around three sides of the house. The small spaces in-between the splits would be later filled with clay. The manicole strips would also be used for the floor, along with jute bags to serve as rugs to prevent splinters from the manicole being lodged in the foot.

"We gon move in next week-end," Slippery Ochro told him. "We gon build a latrine near the cashew tree over there, so we don't have to use your latrine."

Mohabir was so astonished that he could only repeat, "Near the cashew tree," as Slippery Ochro looked at him with a quizzical smile.

Mohabir walked home slowly, a whirlwind of thoughts in his head. When he opened his back door, he saw Dularie in the kitchen. He noticed that her hair was tied in a knot as she was kneading flour to make roti. "They gon move in next week-end," was all he could say.

"So quick!" Dularie was equally astonished as she stared at him.

"They got people helping them. They only got to put in the posts and a wall and roof, and they can stay inside, and do the rest later. I don't know what pickle we put ourselves in. I never like to *tie bundle*[14] with Slippery Ochro and Phulmattie, and now look what happen."

Dularie felt the same way, but when she saw Mohabir scratching his head, and his face mirroring his concern, she knew that she had to console him. "Wha' done, done. Let them build a small house and stay there. We don't have to mix with them, except to say, *Good morning and good afternoon.*"

Mohabir, at some level, knew what his wife was doing, and was grateful for her concern, but expressed his skepticism. "If you say so," he replied and sat in one of the chairs by the table.

When Dularie finished preparing dinner, the two ate in silence, both partly blaming the other for Slippery Ochro and his wife building a house on their land, while nevertheless recognizing his or her role in the decision. After dinner, Mohabir smoked his pipe on the porch, while Dularie washed the dishes. Through the trees, he saw the outline of Slippery Ochro's house. Slippery Ochro and his friends had departed, but Mohabir knew that they would be back after breakfast the following day.

Only half of the sun was shooting rays up the sky, as the birds chirped their last tunes before settling down for the night. As he puffed on his pipe, Mohabir thought, *Slippery Ochro and Phulmattie moved so fast that we did not have time to change our minds. Wha' hole we dig for ourselves?*

Dularie had her own thoughts as she washed the dishes. *I tell Mohabir that we wouldn't have anything to do with Slippery Ochro and Phulmattie. But I know how pushy both of them can be. They gon live on our land just a few yards away from us. How we gon avoid them? I don't care about myself, but Mohabir work hard, and*

---

[14] Have business with

- 10 -

I know how much he like to help people, but he also like peace. And he so soft that people take advantage of him all the time. Then she thought about the situation some more, and added, *I soft too.*

Mohabir and Dularie said little to each other for the remainder of the evening. As they changed into their night clothes earlier than usual, and went to bed that night, their brains were racked with thoughts of Slippery Ochro and Phulmattie being their neighbors, but neither said anything, because each of them did not want to disturb the other. After about an hour of twisting and turning, they both fell asleep.

At about three in the morning, Dularie heard Mohabir thrashing and groaning in his sleep and she shook him awake. "Why you groaning for?"

Mohabir sat up and reached for the towel hanging on the bed board, wiped the sweat off his face, and tried to bring his breathing back to normal. "You know that mango tree which fall down by the path leading to the farm? I dream that I pass there, and a *labaria*[15] bite me."

Dularie sat up, and put her arm around her husband. "You worried about Slippery Ochro and Phulmattie," she said soothingly. "Don't worry. Leh them build their house and stay. We won't have anything to do with them." Even as she said the words, she knew in her heart that they weren't true.

Mohabir, still breathing rapidly, kissed his wife on the top of her head. "Okay! We shouldn'a let them build their house on our land in the first place. But what done, done! We won't have anything to do with them anymore."

Dularie thought, *Who we fooling?* However, she told her husband, "Let we go back to sleep now," as she hugged Mohabir and coaxed him to lie down.

**

The following morning, both were in high spirits as they convinced themselves that they would be able to keep out of the way of Slippery Ochro and his wife. Just as they finished breakfast, and were having their second cup of coffee, they heard a knock at the back door which led to the kitchen. Mohabir and Dularie looked at each other, fear and doubt clouding their faces.

---

[15] A small venomous snake

After a few seconds, Mohabir told his wife, "I don't know who gon knock so early in the morning."

"I scared that it *that* man and his wife. I gon go and see."

Dularie reluctantly went to the door. When she opened it, she was greeted by a wide smile from Phulmattie, who had a cup in her hand. "Dularie gal, I come to borrow a cup of sugar. We move last night, even though the roof na finished. We gon put in the roof later. We went to Manbahal to buy some sugar on credit and he refuse us. Dem shopkeeper get rich off us, and when we ask them for credit, they refuse us. Manbahal don't give you full weight, you know. You look at his scale. He gat it at fifteen ounce, not sixteen ounce."

Phulmattie stretched out her cup, while Dularie stepped back. Phulmattie had neglected to brush her teeth that morning, and her morning breath assaulted Dularie's nostrils. Dularie realized that distancing herself from Phulmattie could have been misinterpreted as her being scornful, so she took the cup from Phulmattie's hand.

"Okay," was all that she could manage. Then she walked to the kitchen where Mohabir was waiting, anxious to hear what transpired. "Slippery Ochro and Phulmattie move in last night. They gon put the roof up later. Phulmattie want to borrow a cup of sugar," Dularie told her husband somewhat mechanically as she filled the cup with sugar. Both husband and wife acknowledged to themselves that *borrow* was a euphemistic term, because many of their friends had *borrowed* money from them. None had repaid the loan.

Both of them thought, *What's a cup of sugar? We can afford it. But it not going to end here.*

Dularie took the cup of sugar to the door and handed it to Phulmattie.

"Thank you, gal! It so good to have nice neighbor like you," Phulmattie said as she smiled and turned to walk down the stairs.

Dularie did not close the door immediately, but looked at Phulmattie as she strutted her way to her roofless hut. *So we're neighbor now? I don't like where this going. But I won't tell Mohabir anything. I don't want to bother him.*

When she went in the kitchen, she found her coffee cold. Luckily, the fire was still going, and there was some coffee left in the pot, so she poured another cup for herself, added milk and sugar, and returned to the table to sit with her husband, who had already finished his coffee, but was waiting for her, expecting some sort of report. Dularie said, "I give she the sugar."

"Tomorrow she gon want salt," her husband predicted.

Although Dularie made a resolution not to share her concerns with her husband, she could not help telling Mohabir, "She say that we neighbor now."

Mohabir got up and started scratching his head and pacing the floor. "First, they ask us to let them build a house on our land. Now, like they own the land, and we neighbors. Next, they gon want us to give them this house and move into the house they build. But what we gon do? *Boat gone ah falls. It can't turn back.*"[16]

"Lord Shiva gon guide us to do the right thing," Dularie replied placatingly.

"I gon go and weed that piece in the coffee farm that the laborers did not weed," Mohabir replied, feeling the need to do something to ease the knot in his stomach. "You want me to pull out some cassava and eddoes, and bring a bunch of plantain so that you can cook some soup this afternoon?"

"Yes! We can cook soup. When Sunilall pass with fish, I gon buy some. Conservancy water low, and people catching fish like crazy."

"I gon tell Sookhu to make a *cast net*[17] for me, so I can go catch some," Mohabir remarked as he went in the bedroom to change his clothes."

"You saying that since we get married, and still no cast net. Now you too old to go and throw net. When we want fish, we gon buy."

Mohabir knew that Dularie was speaking the truth, and just smiled as he changed into his work clothes, took his cutlass, and headed off to his coffee farm.

Dularie busied herself with her household tasks. When she was finished sweeping the kitchen, she gathered the clothes she had put aside for washing and went by the side of the house to the standpipe, which was newly installed, and had a broad piece of board and a *beater*[18] beside it.

Previously, everybody on the south side of the canal had to fetch water from one of the standpipes located on the north side, where the road was located. However, the village council decided to install water pipes on the south side, and also led the pipes into the yards of the residents, so that every household had at least one standpipe on the property. This was a luxury, and some people who could afford it, installed pipelines in their

---

[16] It's too late to change things
[17] Fishing net
[18] A heavy piece of board used to beat the dirt out of clothes

kitchens which enabled them to have sinks and running water. Some others installed shower rooms in their yards, so they could shower in private instead of having to bathe at the standpipe with a bucket and a calabash.

As soon as Dularie sat on the low stool and soaked the clothes, she noticed a shadow beside her, and when she looked up there was Phulmattie in all her gold toothed splendor.

"Heh, eh gal, you washing clothes?"

"Yes! Ah used to wash clothes every day, but since the children married and move out, I only wash every other day now."

"I got some of Slippery Ochro clothes and my dresses to wash. When you finish, can you leave yuh beater so I can wash them. And leave yuh soap too. Ah didn't get to buy *salt-soap*[19] yet."

Dularie looked at Phulmattie like a bird being hypnotized by a snake.

"Thank you, gal. It so nice to have neighbor like you," Phulmattie told Dularie, smiling, her gold teeth flashing in the sun, as she returned to her still roofless house, leaving the frustrated Dularie hitting the clothes furiously with the beater.

Dularie finished washing the clothes, and after hanging them on the line in the yard, returned to the kitchen to prepare rice, dholl, and three fried eggs for lunch for herself and Mohabir. She washed the rice and put it in the pot, her mind in turmoil, and she thought, *Mohabir and me use to live so nice and peaceful. Now we let Slippery Ochro and his wife build a house on our property, and they won't leave us alone. We like to help people, but we too soft, and people take advantage of us.* Then she tried to console herself. *Let Phulmattie use the salt soap. How much soap she gon use? But I know that she gon want to borrow more things. What pugatory[20] we put ourselves in?*

Dularie talked herself into some sort of calm as she prepared lunch. She knew that Mohabir would return home at about noon, eat lunch and then nap for an hour before resuming his afternoon's activities. Lunch was ready when she saw Mohabir, dressed in his old khaki trousers which was torn at the knees, and a long-sleeved plaid shirt, walking home along the path. As usual, he was wearing his wide brimmed straw hat, on which he carried a basket containing some plantains, cassava, eddoes and dasheen, ingredients for the soup they would have for dinner. They would have to

---

[19] Soap used for washing clothes
[20] Purgatory

do without the fish, because Sunilall did not ride past on his bicycle, ringing his bell, and shouting, *FISH FOR SALE! HOURI! PATWA! LUKANANI!*"

However, they had enough ingredients for the soup to be tasty and nutritious, and Dularie thought that she would add some of the salt-fish she had not used for some time because of the availability of fresh fish. She expected Mohabir to be tired. He had slowed down quite a bit lately, but as she saw him walking dejectedly with his head down, she knew that something was bothering him, and waited patiently for him to come home and unburden himself to her. She hurriedly dished out lunch for both and put the plates on the table, looking forward to eating lunch with her husband. She enjoyed these occasions, especially after their children got married and left home. This was the time the two of them talked about their struggles and their triumphs, and reflected how far they had come since they were married.

Mohabir came into the kitchen, threw his hat on a chair, and told his wife, "Somebody cut a hand of plantain from the farm. And they pull out some cassava and eddoes."

"You know when Chaman and his friends do a bush cook, they always take some provision from we farm to put in their soup," Dularie replied, although she had suspicions that it was not Chaman and his friends who raided their farm.

Mohabir thought for a moment before he replied. "Chaman and his friends didn't do no bush cook. Chaman not even home. He gone to spend time with his *mamoo*[21] in Leguan."

Husband and wife looked at each other, and the very real possibility of who took the provisions from their farm dawned on them. "Slippery Ochro!" they said simultaneously. Then they were speechless for a while.

Mohabir broke the silence. "When you get a donkey fuh[22] ride, you should ride it on a good road, not in trench and swamp," he said reflectively.

Although Dularie was concerned about the way things were progressing between Slippery Ochro, Phulmattie and themselves, she wanted to calm her husband, who was always nice to people, and foolishly expected people to respond in kind. She knew that Mohabir became very upset when others did not reciprocate his kindness, but instead took advantage of him. She had frequently pointed out to him, "You live in the perfect world in yuh

---

[21] Maternal uncle
[22] Meaning "to ride"

mind, and expect everybody to behave like you. Not everybody think like you."

When Mohabir had told her about the missing plantain and cassava, she knew that he resented being taken advantage of, and decided to soothe him. "One hand plantain, and two root cassava and some eddoes won't make us poor," she observed, as she put her arm on his shoulder.

"No, but it won't stop there. That is the thin part of the wedge," her husband predicted as he and Dularie sat down to eat lunch. They looked at each other without saying anything, but each knew what the other was thinking.

After lunch, Mohabir showered and went to have a nap, while Dularie soaked some salt fish in water to get rid of the excess salt. She was extremely careful to monitor Mohabir's salt intake since Dr. Singh had told Mohabir that he had high blood pressure, and that he should reduce his intake of salt.

Chapter 2

I drink to make other people more interesting."

—Ernest Hemingway—

Mohabir woke up from his nap at about 2:30 and went to the grove of orange trees behind the house. Oranges in various stages of ripening were hanging from most of the trees, but bird vines were taking over a particular tree, threatening to strangle it. *If I don't get rid of those bird vines, that tree gon die. And it bear sweet oranges.* After looking to ensure that Dularie was not around, he started to climb the tree. He had barely reached the second branch, when he heard Dularie's atypical high-pitched voice.

"Mohabir, you come down from that tree right now. Yuh think yuh young. You too old fuh climb tree. You want fall down and break your ass. Then I got to look after you."

Mohabir did not argue, and climbed down carefully. He told Dularie, "The bird vine take over the tree. If I don't pull them out, they gon kill the tree."

Dularie countered immediately , "Better the tree dead than you dead." Then her voice softened as she exhorted her husband, "When Chaman come home, we gon ask him to climb the tree and pull out the bird vine. He gon be glad to work for some small change. You got to realize that you can't do the things you used to do when you been young. Let the young people do the work. We can afford to pay them."

Mohabir gave the bird vines a malevolent look, but had to accept that Dularie was right. "I used to be able to do all those things when I been younger. I still think that I can do them, but when I try, my body tell me something different," he confessed to Dularie, as he smiled ruefully.

"We all get old, and we can't do the things we use to do when we been young," she told him consolingly. "I, too, can't do the things I use to do when I been young. Let the young people take over from us. We work hard enough in our younger days."

"All right! But we gon ask him as soon as he come back home. You know that that orange tree bear the sweetest orange. That's why I don't sell orange from that tree. The orange from that tree is only for us, or when family come."

"Okay, I gon ask Chaman when he come home." Dularie put her arm on his shoulder. "But you got to promise me that you won't climb any orange tree again. I don't want anything to happen to you. Is me and you alone in this house, and if anything should happen to you, how I gon live in this house alone?"

Mohabir was overcome with emotion and consoled his wife. "All right! I won't climb any tree anymore. Let Chaman do it when he come home. Let Slippery Ochro take any vegetable and fruit he want to eat and cook. But not to sell. What we want at our age? We eat our three meal a day. We got somewhere to rest our head when night come. We got each for company. What more we want?"

Dularie smiled. "We just want to live the rest of our days in peace," she said as she held his hand and they walked under the house where they, like most people in the village, had a hammock slung.

Mohabir lay in the hammock and Dularie sat on one of the chairs near him. They had a number of chairs and a table under the house, and they liked to entertain friends there—in addition to the increased air flow, they could see all around them, and felt freer. As they relaxed in the company of each other, they felt an aura of peace with themselves and the world.

That feeling was abruptly shattered by Slippery Ochro and his wife. "Look at the two of you love birds," Slippery Ochro said as he came under the bottom house. Slippery Ochro wore a straw hat, and the waist of his torn khaki pants was held up by a strong vine, while Phulmattie's red and white flowered dress were hitched to her waist. She, too, wore a straw hat. Uninvited, the two sat in the chairs nearest to Mohabir and Dularie. Slippery Ochro had a large bottle of Russian Bear rum in his hand, and his wife had a packet of Bristol cigarettes in her left hand. Both were smiling and appeared as if they didn't have a care in the world.

"Them boys gon put on the roof this week-end, and I say that we can take a lil drink to celebrate," Slippery Ochro said as he put the bottle on the coffee table.

Where he get money to buy rum? Mohabir thought. *And Phulmattie smoke like a chimney. Where they get money to buy all the cigarette? Dularie and me got some money, but we don't spend it on rum and cigarette.*

Dularie said, "Mohabir don't drink too much. Sometimes, he take one drink before dinner, but he don't drink rum fuh sport."

Phulmattie said, "I agree with you, gal, but this one time we gon take a drink to celebrate everything." She sensed Dularie's hesitation, and added, "We women gon take a finey[23] too. Not only men can drink and smoke. Look how hard we women work. We go and pick coffee whole day, and then come home and cook and clean, while the men drink. We slaves? We can take a drink too."

Dularie was confused. She had never heard of Phulmattie going to pick coffee, or weed the coffee farm with anybody, and guessed that she was talking about other women. But she was also confused about drinking with Slippery Ochro and Phulmattie. In the past, Mohabir often poured a shot glass of rum and handed it to her before dinner. It made her feel good, and increased her appetite, but she never drank with anybody else. She looked at her husband, who had already gotten up to get the glasses from the kitchen.

"Okay! We gon take a small drink before dinner," Mohabir said. When he was halfway up the stairs, he stopped, turned back and warned Phulmattie, "But don't encourage Dularie to start smoking."

Mohabir went to the kitchen and got four glasses and a bottle of Coke which he placed on the table. Slippery Ochro opened the bottle of Russian Bear rum, and took a pocketknife from his back pocket to remove the plastic from the inside of the cork.

"If we lucky, we gon get another bottle for free," he said. At that time, the company distilling Russian Bear rum had a sales promotion, and imprinted a picture of a bear, which was the logo of the brand, on the inside of the cork of selected bottles. Anyone who was lucky to find the logo would get a free bottle of Russian Bear rum. When Slippery Ochro managed to get the circular plastic disk out from the cork, he laughed loudly. "We got a bottle of free rum," he shouted, as he showed the likeness of a bear in the cork.

Mohabir was both happy and concerned. While he thoroughly enjoyed a drink with Dularie before dinner, he was not comfortable with his wife sitting down with Slippery Ochro and Phulmattie drinking, and wished that Slippery Ochro had brought a half bottle —mickey—instead. He looked around the table, his face mirroring his concern.

Slippery Ochro reassured him. "Don't worry, Mohabir. The women work hard, and it not fair for us men to drink and...". Slippery Ochro was on the verge of saying "drink and smoke," but he remembered Mohabir's

---

[23] Small bottle of liquor

exhortations to Phulmattie just in time, and continued "have a nice time. Besides, we home. We not in any rum shop, where anybody can take their eyes pass her."

Phulmattie said, "Dularie, girl, it better if we take a drink with we husbands. Look how nice we sit down here. Other women go to the kitchen and drink *hide-hide*, and then come out and pretend that they didn't drink anything. We sit down nice and peaceful in we house and take a drink and talk with we husbands."

With that, she grabbed the bottle, and poured liberal amounts for everybody.

Mohabir and Dularie, feeling powerless, looked at each other, until Phulmattie finished pouring rum and Coke in all the glasses.

Slippery Ochro told Mohabir, "I cut a hand plantain from one of your tree this morning. And I pull out two root cassava and some eddo to make soup. I don't know if you cook dinner yet Dularie, but Phulmattie, after you take this drink, go and bring the pot of soup over and we can all eat right here." He laughed loudly. "After all, it Mohabir provisions we cook."

Mohabir and Dularie remained mesmerized, and automatically raised their glasses and drank with Slippery Ochro and Phulmattie. After the first drink, Dularie noticed that her head was feeling lighter, and was surprised when Phulmattie left and *walked straight as an arrow* to her house. They lost sight of her once she walked into the coffee trees, but were not worried, although the sun was already setting.

"I might as well light the lamps in the meantime," Dularie told her husband. Like most people in the village, Dularie was superstitious regarding the lighting of lamps, and considered it bad luck for darkness to fall without at least one lamp being lit in the house.

"I gon light the gas lamp and bring it downstairs," Mohabir told her.

After he lit the lamp in the kitchen, Dularie left her husband who was in the process of lighting the *Petromax*, which would give a brighter light than the lantern, which they usually lit when they were downstairs. She almost tripped on the third step, and had to hold on to the rails for the remainder of the way down. As she made her way to her chair, Phulmattie emerged from the coffee trees, holding a large pot. The aroma of the soup was pleasant to Dularie's nostrils, and she temporarily forgot about her concerns regarding Slippery Ochro and Phulmattie.

"I gon bring soup bowls and spoons," Dularie said, and made her way into the kitchen.

"I gon help you with the plates," Phulmattie volunteered, and started to follow her.

Dularie did not want Phulmattie in her kitchen, and was unsure whether she was too kind or too scared to tell her that she did not want any help, so she complacently allowed Phulmattie to accompany her in the kitchen. She handed Phulmattie four bowls from a shelf, and then opened a drawer and selected four spoons. By then, Mohabir had finished lighting the Petromax, and was on his way downstairs through the kitchen, the gas lamp emitting a bright white light.

When they were all seated, Phulmattie told Mohabir, as he hung the lamp on a nail in one of the beams of the house, "You light lamp early."

"I like to light the lamp before it get dark. "So no darkness can enter the house, before we sleep."

Phulmattie smiled as she opened the pot which was three quarters full of soup, with thick, rich gravy. As they dished it in their plates, Mohabir was surprised to see fish in it.

"Where you get fish from?" he asked Slippery Ochro.

"Mohan been a conservancy to catch fish and he give me a large *houri*[24]. I cut it up in four pieces, so each of us can get one piece." Before they started eating, Slippery Ochro held up his glass and told Mohabir, "Leh[25] we tek[26] a drink before we eat. I glad that you let us build our house on your land. If anybody want to take their eyes pass you, you tell me. I gon light a fire up their ass. I representing you now."

Mohabir did not feel that he needed any representation, because he largely minded his own business and got along well with everybody in the village, but he acknowledged Slippery Ochro's statement by saying, "Thank you!"

They all raised their glasses, before turning their attention to their plates. The soup was delicious. Phulmattie had allowed the eddoes to boil until they became very soft and blended with the gravy. The spinach she added in liberal amounts made the gravy thick and tasty. Three bright uncut peppers, which floated on the gravy, added a tang to the soup, while not making it too hot. While Dularie found the soup very delicious, she also remembered the doctor telling Mohabir not to eat too much pepper

---

[24] A tropical fish similar to the pike
[25] Let
[26] take

because of his hemorrhoids, but was relieved when she saw that none of it ended up in his plate.

Dularie knew that the plantains, eddoes and cassava came from her farm, but could not figure where Phulmattie got the spinach and peppers from. Then she remembered that Dhanraj, their neighbor on the west side, had planted peppers and spinach in his garden, and figured that Slippery Ochro and Phulmattie must have wangled some from him. Even as she enjoyed the soup, she thought, *They know how to get things from people.*

By the time everybody had finished eating the soup, the bottle of rum was almost finished.

Slippery Ochro poured drinks only for himself and Mohabir, explaining to the women, "You all had more than enough to drink. Mohabir and I gon finish the bottle."

If he thought that he could deprive Phulmattie of the last drink, he was wrong. Phulmattie quickly countered with, "I gon drink some of yuh drink. I don't want you to drink too much and get drunk." She took a large gulp before returning the glass to her husband.

Mohabir and Dularie looked at each other and smiled. Then Mohabir asked his wife, "You want drink some of this?" as he held out his glass.

"Me head swinging already," Dularie said. "You know I not accustomed to drinking so much. You, too, don't drink so much." When they were finished eating, Dularie got up to take the dishes to the kitchen, then sat back down immediately, closed her eyes, and told her husband, "Me head going round and round."

"It because you not accustomed to drinking," Phulmattie told her. "I gon take the dishes to the kitchen. You stay and rest a bit." Phulmattie gathered the plates and attempted to hold the glasses also, but discovered that she was unable to hold both the glasses and the plates. "Mohabir, you bring the glasses, and then you can help Dularie go upstairs."

Mohabir grabbed the four glasses and followed Phulmattie up the stairs. They went into the kitchen and Phulmattie put the plates in the sink, which was outside the window, allowing the water to drain directly on the ground. She stood beside the window, and when Mohabir reached to put the glasses and plates into the sink, she pretended to reach for one of the plates, and her hand brushed against his. When Mohabir felt Phulmattie's breasts pressed against him, he glanced over his shoulder, and saw her gold teeth flashing in the light of the wall lamp in the kitchen. He was at a loss on how to respond. On the one hand, he was flattered that a woman found a man his age attractive. But he was not accustomed to a woman being the aggressor. In his mind, the man should be the hunter and pursue his prey. If Phulmattie is the aggressor, then who was he? They both heard Slippery Ochro's footsteps on the stairs, and they both took a few guilty steps apart, as they looked at each other—partners in crime.

"I just come to see if you need any help," Slippery Ochro said as he came in the kitchen. "Dularie fall asleep in the chair."

"We just coming downstairs," Phulmattie replied as she moved towards the door—Mohabir and Slippery Ochro close behind.

The sight of Dularie slumped on the chair was a strange sight to Mohabir, who had never seen his wife like that in all the years they had been married.

"She just tired," Phulmattie assured him. "We gon go home now. You help Dularie walk up the step." Then she rested her hand on Mohabir's arm. "You don't let her fall down the stairs now," she cautioned as she gave Mohabir's hand a squeeze, before she and her husband made their way to their house.

Mohabir held his wife by the shoulder and urged, "Get up now, Dularie. I think that Slippery Ochro and his wife force you to drink too much. You not accustomed to drink so much. I gon help you up the stairs and you can go to sleep. You gon feel better in the morning."

Dularie leaned on her husband's shoulder and stood up with great effort. Mohabir half carried her up the stairs and led her to the bedroom where she collapsed on the bed, and fell asleep without putting on her nightie. Mohabir also felt a bit wobbly, but managed to slip out of his clothes and wear his pajamas before lying down beside Dularie, who was snoring heavily. Mohabir remembered her telling him how much he snored whenever he drank.

As he lay in bed, Mohabir reviewed the events of the day. He thought that, before Slippery Ochro and Phulmattie moved in, he would normally take a drink or two, and Dularie would take one drink, which he would have poured for her, and then they would eat dinner. But Slippery Ochro and his wife changed all that with the bottle of Russian Bear rum that they brought. Then he remembered that Slippery Ochro won another bottle of rum, and in spite of what happened that evening, he found himself hoping that Slippery Ochro would bring the bottle he won so that they would drink it together.

He looked at his wife, intoxicated, and wondered why he wanted Slippery Ochro to bring another bottle. Then he remembered the soft touch of Phulmattie's breast on his shoulder, her seductive gold-toothed smile, and the boost to his ego that he *still had it*. As he started to nod off, he thought that the life he and Dularie had was peaceful, but he rationalized that it was so peaceful that it was dull, and told himself that it was perhaps a good thing that Slippery Ochro and Phulmattie asked to build a house on their land.

Perhaps I need some excitement at this stage in my life, he thought as he drifted off to sleep.

Mohabir was awakened at about 2:00 in the morning by the sound of retching, and he raised his head and looked at Dularie who was still lying down, but with her head over the side of the bed. She was holding her stomach with her right hand, and was vomiting directly onto the wood floor. Mohabir sat up and started to rub her back as he thought that the last time that he saw his wife vomiting was when she was pregnant with their second child. *I can't blame her. I encourage her to drink with Slippery Ochro and his wife,* he thought.

Dularie must have read his thoughts. Between bouts of vomiting she admonished her husband, "You make me drink too much."

"Yes! You not accustomed to drinking," he consoled. "You want me to make a cup tea for you?"

"If I drink tea, I gon only vomit more. I want to sleep now."

**

When they woke up in the morning, Dularie was too embarrassed to look her husband in his eyes. She filled a bucket with water, took a rag and cleaned the vomit on her side of the bed. It was not a new task. Occasionally when family or friends visited, Mohabir drank too much and he would vomit. When their two sons were living with them, they frequently drank a lot and vomited on the floor during the night. Although she was suffering from a terrible hangover, Dularie smiled as she remembered her sons blaming each other for vomiting on the floor. For her, though, cleaning her own *rum vomit* was a new experience, and she was wondering how Mohabir would react.

There was no need for her to worry. When she was finished cleaning the floor, she walked through the kitchen to empty the bucket. Mohabir was cooking roti and frying potatoes and bora.

Mohabir looked at his wife and was astonished. Dularie's eyes were red, her face puffed, and her hair was disheveled. She was still wearing the rumpled clothes she had slept in, and was looking at the floor, too embarrassed to make eye contact with her husband.

Mohabir was also wrestling with his own embarrassment for encouraging his wife to drink. However, he was also feeling slightly euphoric, and could still feel the softness of Phulmattie's breast against his shoulder. "Everything okay," he told his wife. "Slippery Ochro and Phulmattie happy that we allow them to build their house on our land, and they just want to have a drink with us and thank us."

Dularie accepted her husband's explanation gratefully, and sat at the kitchen table while Mohabir brought food and coffee and sat down to join her. After a few mouthfuls and a cup of coffee, Dularie gathered enough courage to talk about what happened. "First time I drink so much. But after I take two drinks, it make me feel nice, and I want to drink more."

"Rum don't tell you to stop," Mohabir observed.

This was the only conversation they had as they ate breakfast in silence, stealing quick glances at each other.

**

It reminded Mohabir of the first time they saw each other at a wedding in No. 63 village on the East Coast, when Mohabir had attended a *bariat*.[27] His friend, Dilip, was getting married, and Mohabir was drinking rum with his friends when he saw a fair, slender girl dressed in a red sari with gold embroidery at the edges. Mohabir was glad that he had cut his hair, wore his blue serge pants and the one Arrow *drip dry* shirt that he possessed. He was grateful that he spent about half an hour polishing his black moccasins to a shine. Mohabir and Dularie looked shyly at each other for a few seconds, then turned away and would again sneak quick glances at each other. This continued for a while, with Mohabir becoming bolder and staring longer after he saw Dularie smiling at him.

One of the village women, who happened to be Dularie's aunt, approached Mohabir and asked him, "Why you boring that girl with your eyes?"

"Auntie, she very beautiful. She married?"

"No!" Dularie's aunt replied. "You want married she? I can ask home for her."

---

[27] Wedding party

"I live in Canal No. 2. Same village as Dilip. Ask her if she like me. Her parents can come to Canal and ask for Mohabir. Everybody in the village know my dad. Then they can *ask home for me*.[28] Mohabir and Dularie got married five months later, and raised two strong, handsome sons who got married and moved to their own homes.

**

Now, thirty-five years later, they were playing the same game, but only because Dularie drank too much the previous night.

After breakfast, Mohabir announced, "I gon start weeding the coffee walk. I gon start at the end and weed toward the house, so every day I gon have to walk less."

Although she was hung-over, Dularie decided to assert herself. "Why don't you hire some laborers? We got money to pay them. What you gon do with the money? You can't take it with you."

"I gon work only half day every day, and then I gon come home and rest." Then a thought suddenly occurred to Mohabir, and he asked Dularie, "Why don't I hire Slippery Ochro for half a day every day. He live right here on our land?"

Dularie put her hand on her head. This time it was not because of her headache. "Bhapray! What ants' nest you want stir up, now? What you see in broad daylight, yuh gon light candle to see nighttime?"

Mohabir decided to end his wife's tirade. "Slippery Ochro won't work anyway. You ever see him work with anybody? I don't know why I say I gon ask him to help me. Maybe because he staying on our land."

This seemed to placate Dularie, who was starting to feel better. "If you want to start to weed the coffee walk, fine. But only work half day. And when you get tired, stop. We gon pay dem boys to weed the rest. Dem young. I gon put some water in a bottle and pack up a little bit of roti and the potato and bora so that you can eat a little when you get hungry."

Mohabir smiled as he went to the bedroom to put on his work clothes. In preparation for the weeding, he sat on the back steps and started to sharpen his cutlass. He thought that he would give it a really good sharpening before starting out to the coffee walk and sharpen it again quickly whenever he stopped to rest. As he rubbed the file against the edge of his cutlass, he saw Slippery Ochro on one of the tangerine trees.

---

[28] Propose marriage

Through a curious coincidence, his and Slippery Ochro's eyes *made four,*[29] and Slippery Ochro raised his hand in greeting. Mohabir also raised his right hand, which contained the file. He was only slightly upset that Slippery Ochro was picking some of his tangerines, because he expected that Slippery Ochro would pick his fruits sooner or later. Kandhai always paid more for tangerines, because they were sweeter than oranges, and unlike oranges, they could be peeled without a knife.

Mohabir accepted Slippery Ochro's reaping of his citrus with resignation. Life had been good to him. He had no debts, and had some savings in the bank. "A few tangerines won't make me poor," he said aloud to himself as he continued to sharpen his cutlass.

He was almost finished, when he heard footsteps approaching, and when he looked up, he saw Slippery Ochro coming up the steps with four big, ripe tangerines in his hand.

"I bring some for you and Dularie," Slippery Ochro said. "You know, you got so many orange and tangerine trees, but I never see you and Dularie eating any. It good for you."

Mohabir put his cutlass and file down, accepted the tangerines, and got up to go to the kitchen to give them to Dularie. As he made his way up the stairs, he thought, *He right! Dularie and me should eat more orange and tangerine. But it look like he and Phulmattie gon eat more of our orange and tangerine than we.*

When he went into the kitchen, Dularie was sweeping the floor with a coconut broom. She stopped and straightened up as she saw Mohabir.

"Slippery Ochro pick some tangerine and he bring some for us," Mohabir told her as he gave her the tangerines.

Dularie was in a puckish mood that morning, and replied, "He so nice to give we tangerines. Where he get it from?"

Mohabir laughed, as he turned and went to rejoin Slippery Ochro by the steps.

---

[29] Met

Chapter 3

"Between men and women there is no friendship possible. There is passion, enmity, worship, love, but no friendship."

—Oscar Wilde—

When Mohabir went downstairs, he saw Slippery Ochro holding his cutlass, passing his finger along its edge. "This cutlass so sharp, it can cut iron," he told Mohabir. "What you gon do with it?"

"Oh! I gon start weeding the coffee walk. I gon make a start before we hire people to weed it. I gon work only half day, and come home when I tired."

"You alone going, or Dularie going with you?"

"I alone going. Dularie staying home to do the housework."

"She should go with you to keep you company. You never can tell what can happen. You can cut yourself. Snake can bite you. If somebody with you, they can help you."

Mohabir had never considered this before, and had always been content to go to the coffee walk and farm alone, and leave Dularie to do the cooking and housework, knowing that he would have a hot meal when he came home. *How come Dularie never think of that?* he asked himself. *She care what happen to me?* Then he felt guilty about having such thoughts about his wife, and remembered that, when he came home, he never had to worry about anything.

"I would'a come with you, but Gobin ask me to help him bring some timber. He borrow Seegol bull to pull the *ballahoo*[30] and timber, but he need somebody to stay in the boat and steer it. It not hard work, and I tell him I gon do it. I gon send Phulmattie to work with you for half day. If she can't

---

[30] Small wooden boat

- 28 -

work hard, at least she can keep you company." Slippery Ochro spoke in such a manner that Mohabir was not even aware that he had a choice, and he passively accepted that Phulmattie would accompany him. The memory of Phulmattie's breast against his shoulder the previous night, likely influenced his agreement to her company.

What will Dularie say? he thought. *How can I tell her, so that she will not be angry?*

"I gon go and tell Phulmattie to get ready. When you leaving?"

"After I finish sharpen my cutlass," Mohabir replied, still thinking of how to tell Dularie, who joined them at the bottom of the stairs.

Slippery Ochro solved the problem for him, as he turned to Dularie with his signature smile. "Mohabir too old to go alone to weed coffee walk. Anything can happen to him. He can cut himself. Labaria can bite him. He can faint. I gon ask Phulmattie to work with him for half a day. After all, we glad that you and Mohabir let we build we house on your land. We want to help out a little." Then he turned to Mohabir, "You gon come home fuh lunch, right?"

Dularie and Mohabir felt as if they no choice, and acknowledged that Slippery Ochro made some valid points. Mohabir, thinking of the possibilities with Phulmattie, had mixed feelings, and was not sure that he wanted to spit out the hook he had swallowed, but was more concerned about Dularie's reaction.

Dularie thought that Slippery Ochro might be right, and blamed herself for letting Mohabir go alone to work in the farm. *I so lucky nothing happen to him*, she said to herself. *I can go with him, but I not accustomed to hard work.*

Aloud, she said, "You right, Slippery Ochro. I don't know why I allow Mohabir to go to the coffee walk and the farm alone. All of we getting old. But I tell him over and over to hire laborers to work. I tell him that he should just go and see how things are going, but not to work alone."

Slippery Ochro advised Dularie, "If he want to go and work for a little bit, that okay. But somebody should go with him, in case something happen. If he only working for half day, I gon send Phulmattie with him."

Mohabir breathed a sigh of relief, bordering on ecstasy, when Dularie told Slippery Ochro, "All right! I glad that somebody going with him. I shouldn't a let him go alone all this time."

Mohabir picked up his cutlass and continued sharpening it with an extra flourish, while Slippery Ochro hurried home to tell his wife about the new task for which he volunteered her.

Dularie retreated to the kitchen to prepare water and snacks for Mohabir and Phulmattie.

About half an hour later, Mohabir saw Phulmattie making her way through the coffee trees. She wore an old straw hat, and one side of her red and yellow petticoat was tucked over her waist. The toes of her right foot protruded from a large hole in her black long-boots, which most people wore to work on their farms to protect themselves from thorns and snake bites.

"I see you sharpen your cutlass already. Can you sharpen mine for me?" She handed a thin cutlass, with a dull edge to Mohabir, while proudly displaying her gold teeth.

"This cutlass can't cut butter on a hot day," Mohabir told her, as he ran his finger along the edge. "When last you sharpen it?"

"I can't remember. I ask Slippery Ochro to sharpen it a long time ago, but you know how he stay. He always say he gon do it, but he never do." Phulmattie looked at Mohabir seductively.

Mohabir took the cutlass from her and started rubbing the file against its edges.

Dularie heard the conversation between her husband and Phulmattie and joined them, a rum bottle full of water in one hand, and a covered saucepan with rice and vegetables in the other. She had packed extra food when she learned that Phulmattie would be accompanying her husband. "I pack some food for the two of you," she told her husband. "One bottle of water gon be enough for you. When it finish, you can come home."

She stayed with Mohabir and Phulmattie until Mohabir had sharpened Phulmattie's cutlass to a fine edge.

"You got to sharpen it often," he told her. "Don't wait until it get dull. Otherwise, it gon take a long time to sharpen."

"I so glad that you sharpen it for me. We don't have any file. I gon borrow yuh file sometimes and sharpen it." She turned to Dularie. "I can help you weed around the house then."

They like man and wife, Dularie thought. as she watched Phulmattie walking beside her husband on the narrow pathway, her hand sometimes brushing against Mohabir's. Dularie was still not feeling one hundred percent after drinking so much the previous night, and was wondering how Phulmattie could feel so chippy and energetic. As she looked with envy at the figure beside her husband, she realized that Phulmattie probably drank frequently, and had developed some resistance to alcohol. *But I don't want to become like her,* she thought. *I like to take one drink, or two the most, with Mohabir before dinner. But it look like Phulmattie can drink more than some men.*

As she continued to look at them, she wished that Phulmattie would not walk so closely to Mohabir. *She can walk behind him. The path narrow. Why she got to walk beside him?* Her head was full of conflicting thoughts as she watched them until they rounded a bend in the path she then returned to the kitchen to continue her chores.

Although she was busy in the kitchen, Dularie allowed her imagination to run amok, and thought, *Phulmattie gone with Mohabir. I hope Slippery Ochro don't come and ask for anything. I am alone home, and I don't like any man coming here when Mohabir not home.* The feeling of unease stayed with her throughout the morning, although Slippery Ochro was too busy helping Gobin to visit the home in Mohabir's absence.

**

When they reached the furthermost limits of the coffee farm, Mohabir put the bottle of water and snack in the shade of a large jamoon tree. "We gon make a start here," he told Phulmattie. "I gon hire some laborers to weed the whole coffee walk, but I just want to make a start."

"You so good. Most people with some money play big shot and pay laborers to do all the work. But you not too proud to work. Leh we weed before the sun get too hot. Then we can rest a little."

As they cut the saplings among the coffee trees, Mohabir was surprised at the speed and endurance of Phulmattie. He was accustomed to such work, but based on Slippery Ochro's and Phulmattie's lifestyles, he did not expect that Phulmattie was capable of keeping up with him.

After working for an hour, Mohabir told Phulmattie that they should rest a bit and sharpen their cutlasses. They sat under the jamoon tree, and Mohabir was quite pleased when he looked at the amount of work they did. *That how much I expect I would do before I go home,* he thought, as he took Phulmattie's cutlass and began to sharpen it. Phulmattie sat opposite him, her back against the stump of a buxton spice-mango tree, and Mohabir remembered how much Dularie enjoyed the sweet buxton spice mangoes which he brought for her when it was in season. He did not know why the tree died, but he had to cut it down because it was in danger of falling.

Phulmattie's legs were raised at her knees, allowing Mohabir a clear view of her thighs. At first, Mohabir refused to look, focusing instead on her face and the movement of her gullet as she swallowed water from the rum bottle. However, he had to look down to feel the edge of her cutlass he was sharpening, and as his gaze strayed and lingered at her thighs, he expected to see her panties. Instead, he saw a patch of dark hair between her legs, and his hands began to shake as he rubbed his fingers against the edge of the cutlass.

Phulmattie noticed the trembling hands and moved beside him. "Be careful or you gon cut your hand." She smiled mischievously, as she gently took the cutlass from him and laid it carefully on the ground an arm's length away from them. When she rubbed her hand on Mohabir's knee in order to wipe off the sweat on her palms, Mohabir was thrilled by her touch. Since he married Dularie, he had not been this close to another woman, except his mother and his sisters. He leaned back on the jamoon tree as Phulmattie moved her hand further up his thigh. Before he knew it, her fingers were undoing the buttons of his trousers. Mohabir enjoyed being seduced, and thought of how he always had to be the initiator of any intimacy with Dularie.

It never occurred to him to stop Phulmattie from opening the fly of his trousers and stroking him. Born in a man's world, Mohabir was convinced that the man should be the pursuer, and that it would not befit his masculinity to refuse the advances of a female. He put his arms around Phulmattie's shoulders and gently lowered her to the ground. She obliged, while still stroking him, maintaining his arousal. Experience had taught her that a man with an erection could be handled as easily as a child who has been offered candy.

As Mohabir mounted her, she moaned in pleasure, and in one fluid movement maneuvered herself on top of him. As he lay beneath Phulmattie, Mohabir thought of how Dularie was never this aggressive, and although she was always willing, she was often non-participatory, as if the act was solely for his benefit. With Phulmattie working vigorously on top of him, he was exposed for the first time in his life to the notion that women can possibly enjoy sex too, and felt proud that he could give pleasure to Phulmattie.

Afterwards, as they lay on the ground, Phulmattie turned to him and said, "You good, you know. Slippery Ochro drink too much rum. It make him soft like pap."

Mohabir, unaware that he was being manipulated, proudly told Phulmattie, "You like it? I glad."

"Not because of this one time, you gon take advantage of me, now. Slippery Ochro always helping people, and he want me to help you work in the farm, because it not safe for you to work alone. But I don't want you to use this excuse to do it every time you alone with me."

She held Mohabir's hand and looked him in the eyes. "Promise me that you won't take advantage of me every time we come to the backdam[31]," but the twinkle in her eyes, and her mischievous smile belied her words.

Mohabir didn't know how to reply. Phulmattie had been the aggressor, but now she was asking him not to take advantage of her in the future. He felt a tinge of guilt for being unfaithful for the first time since he married Dularie. The only words that he could think of were, "Make sure you don't tell Dularie anything."

"You think I stupid? But I don't want you to drink and tell Slippery Ochro anything. I know when people drink, their mouth run like river water."

For years, Mohabir would wonder why he made the next comment. "If you give me whenever I want, I promise not to tell nobody nothing."

"Because you get me, you want do it steady or else you gon tell people? I don't want people to spoil my character, so I gon give you when you want, but you got to promise not to tell anybody."

In his naivete, Mohabir thought that he just achieved a very important victory. "Deal?" he asked as he stretched out his hand. Phulmattie made an effort not to laugh as she shook his hand. "We weed enough for today. Leh we go home now," Mohabir told her as helped her up.

They walked home in silence, with Mohabir leading the way, his mind filled with muddled thoughts. He had thoroughly enjoyed Phulmattie's assertiveness. For part of the encounter, he just had to lie there and Phulmattie did all the work, something he never enjoyed with Dularie. But then, he thought of Dularie, and wondered whether she would be able to guess what happened. Previously, he had no reason to practice subterfuge, because he had been totally honest in his dealings with her.

I just have to act normal, and be nice to her.. Besides, it was only one time. Then he looked back and glanced at Phulmattie, who was a few steps behind, with a quizzical smile on her face. *But she live on our land. Never mind. No matter what I tell her before, I gon try and keep away from her.*

---

[31] Area lying outside village or town

When they were at his house, Phulmattie branched off to go to her home, and Mohabir went to the standpipe by the side of his house.

Dularie had seen them approaching and went to meet him. "You come home early."

"Oh yes. Phulmattie work like a man. She weed *even and straight* with me, and we did quite a lot." On an impulse, he added, "You know, we can hire her as a laborer. We won't have to pay her as much as we pay dem boys, and we can work only half day every day."

Dularie did not know how to respond. Their few differences of opinion centered around Mohabir working too hard, and not taking enough care of himself, and she focused on that. "Why you want to weed the coffee walk yourself? We can afford to pay laborers to weed it. You remember that the doctor tell you to be careful with your blood pressure. You take your pressure medicine this morning?"

"You see me drink my pressure pill. But the doctor say that a little exercise good for my blood pressure. And I like to go to the farm now and then."

Dularie could not deny any of Mohabir's assertions. He dearly loved his land, and became even more attached to it after he left the sugar-estate, because it then became their *bread and butter*. "All right! But you got to promise not to work more than half-day, and then come home and rest." Then she thought about it and added, "But still hire some laborers. Or at least one. Then you can work with them half day, and leave them to work the full day. Or you can hire them for half day. A lot of them boys like to work half day. Then they got the rest of the day to do what they want."

Mohabir, still feeling guilty about his adventure with Phulmattie, quickly conceded, "All right! I gon ask if one or two of the boys gon work with me half day. What you cook for lunch?" But even as he said it, he was thinking that a laborer or two would interfere with his getting together with Phulmattie.

"Rice and shrimp curry. Wash yuh hands. You come home early, and the rice is still boiling, but it gon be ready soon."

Mohabir went to the standpipe and washed his hands and feet. He really wanted to wash between his legs, because he did not know whether Phulmattie's smell was still on him, but to do so, he would have to go to the bathroom, a simple structure beside the kitchen, and he did not want Dularie to suspect anything. He was so flattered that a woman to whom he was not married would find him attractive that he went directly into the bedroom after washing up, and looked at himself in the mirror. He saw a dignified, mature, mustached gentleman with a kind face looking back at him, and he smiled as he stroked his moustache. Then he thought of the stature that he enjoyed in the village. He was one of the five men who constituted the *Panchayat*,[32] and was pleased that he was partly responsible for the mediation and resolution of many disputes that would have otherwise ended up in the courts. Besides the expenditure of time and money, villagers distrusted the courts and lawyers, whom they frequently called *liars* who charged exorbitant fees, and spoke in legal jargon which few villagers understood.

Then he frowned as he thought, *What if Phulmattie tell Slippery Ochro about us, and Panchayat has to come to my house?* Brows furrowed, he went in the kitchen to talk with Dularie while she prepared their lunch. *I got to act normal*, he thought, as he seated himself at the table. *Dularie like to talk with me while she cooking*.

Dularie greeted him with a smile. "It's a bit early for lunch, but I almost finish. You look tired. I glad that you come home early. You work hard in yuh young days, and you got to take it easy now. Let me just strain the rice and then we can eat."

Perhaps because he was tired, or because he felt guilty, or because of the rum he drank the previous night, Mohabir felt the need for a drink. Dularie never objected to his drinking before dinner, but frequently questioned his drinking so early in the day, so Mohabir decided to blame Slippery Ochro. "Slippery Ochro make we drink too much last night, and I *stale bruise*.[33] I think I gon take a drink before I eat lunch."

Mohabir was surprised by Dularie's response. "I also don't feel like eating because of the drinks last night. Mix a small one for me, and it may make me hungry." Then she made a rare statement as she looked at Mohabir seductively. "When we finish eating, you can have a shower and we can go rest. I bathed this morning, and all the housework finish."

Mohabir was in a quandary. He was unsure whether he would be able to perform with Dularie so soon after his tryst with Phulmattie, and he still experienced a tremendous feeling of guilt, exacerbated by Dularie's sweetness and caring. He replied, "I feel so tired. I just want to take a big drink, shower and sleep." He felt an extra layer of guilt for refusing Dularie's advances and he added, "But I like to sleep near you."

---

[32] Group of elders who mediated conflicts
[33] Have a hangover

This seemed to satisfy Dularie, who had just finished straining the rice. Mohabir had already poured tall drinks in two glasses, and added Pepsi as Dularie dished out rice and shrimp curry, set the plates on the table, and sat down to drink and eat with her husband. They raised their glasses in a salute to each other and drank. Mohabir drank more than half of his in one gulp while Dularie took a small sip. Mohabir could feel the rum burning his gullet as it made its way to his stomach where it produced a warm feeling, and he began to feel better. He looked at his wife, who was taking her first mouthful, and was overwhelmed by emotions of love and gratitude.

I cannot spoil this, he thought. *I cannot let Phulmattie and Slippery Ochro spoil the love and peace I have in my house. I will not have sex with Phulmattie again. She can climb on top of somebody else.*

"Wha' happen? You not eating."

"I think I gon take another drink. Then I gon eat. You want some more?" Mohabir got up to refill his glass.

"What happen with you? You never drink so much at lunch."

Mohabir realized that he was not following his self-imposed rule to *act normal.*

However, he was so anguished and confused that he could not stop himself from having another drink, and consoled Dularie with, "One last drink, and then I gon eat, shower and have a nap. You want another small one?"

"No! I not finished with the one you pour for me. You take another drink and then eat. But don't make it a habit."

Mohabir poured his second drink, returned to the table, and took a few mouthfuls of rice and shrimp curry before again raising his glass to Dularie, who smiled and reached for her glass. They both drank and ate the remainder of their meal in silence, engrossed in their own thoughts. When they were finished, Mohabir rinsed his mouth, while Dularie cleared the table. He went to the bedroom to get his towel, and made his way to the bathroom outside, grateful that he can finally wash Phulmattie off him. As he soaped himself, he felt a sense of relief. Although he had enjoyed the experience, he began to question whether it was worth the guilt he was feeling, and the possible conflict with Dularie. He felt clean as he dried himself and walked back to the house with his towel wrapped around his waist.

Dularie was already changed and in bed, and looked at him half-expectantly when he entered the bedroom, but he deftly slipped his shorts under the towel before he unwrapped it. After putting on his t-shirt he lay beside her, covered himself with the thin flowered sheet, and rolled to his side facing Dularie. As he threw his arm around her waist, he regretted not being able to initiate any intimacy with her after his tryst with Phulmattie. He knew how much Dularie enjoyed their get-togethers at this time, when they would sleep until two or three in the afternoon after their intimacy. Then they each would go about their chores until dinner.

Chapter 4

"It is very normal for one ugly weed to not want to stand alone."

——Suzy Kassem—

Rise Up and Salute the Sun: The Writings of Suzy Kassem

Mohabir liked to be alone to smoke his pipe, and practice his checker game after dinner. He was quite proficient at the game, and many younger men were eager to play with him in Naraine's tailoring establishment, which also housed a modest soft drink and confectionery shop. Naraine kept a checkerboard and the required pieces in the shop, along with packets of cards and dominoes. Fondly referred to as the *Cake Shop* by everybody, it was a favorite meeting place for men in that area, and was only a short walk from Mohabir's home. Sometimes Mohabir got so caught up in the game that he played under the light of Naraine's gas lamp until late in the night. When this happened quite a few successive nights, he decided that after lunch was a better time to be intimate with Dularie. His evenings would then be free.

He and Dularie dozed off until a banging on the door caused Mohabir to raise his head and look at the alarm clock on the dresser. They had bought the alarm clock when he was working at the estate office, and it was still working fine, although they no longer needed the alarm feature. It showed 1:30—well before he and Dularie were ready to get up, but Mohabir got off the bed, put on his trousers, and went to answer the door.

He was greeted by a smiling Slippery Ochro, wearing his usual straw hat, torn trousers and a checkered shirt. "I got the free bottle of Russian Bear," he exclaimed as he proudly brandished an unopened bottle.

Groggy and resentful at having to leave Dularie's side, Mohabir stared at Slippery Ochro, who apparently already had a few drinks.

"Phulmattie gon come over. We gon wait for you and Dularie at the bottom house, and then we gon tek a few."

He inviting me to my own house, Mohabir thought. *What will Dularie say?* Then he remembered the time he spent with Phulmattie and he weakened. "You say that Phulmattie gon join us?"

"Yes! Phulmattie said that the two of you weed quite a bit. I glad that she help you. She showering now, but gon come as soon as she finish. I gon wait for you downstairs." Slippery Ochro held the bottle to his chest, walked down the stairs, and into the bottom house, leaving Mohabir debating how to tell Dularie that their new neighbors invited them for another drink.

Having ensconced himself in the rocking chair which Mohabir had reserved for himself, Slippery Ochro debated whether to open the bottle and have a drink while waiting. He and Gobin had already enjoyed a bottle of Russian Bear, which Gobin had bought in return for his help, and he had hoped that he would find a Russian bear imprinted on the inside of the cork when he opened the bottle, but he was disappointed.

Free rum is the best rum, Slippery Ochro had thought, as he poured for himself and Gobin. Then he thought of Mohabir and Dularie. *Or when you buy rum for somebody, and you get more from them.*

Slippery Ochro leaned back in the rocking chair and smiled at his good fortune. *I got a place where I build me house, and I don't got to pay rent. I can even pick fruit from the trees and I don't got to pay. I so lucky that I even get a free bottle of Russian Bear. I happy to get a wife like Phulmattie. We work together. People help us, and we help them.*

As Slippery Ochro looked at the bottle of Russian Bear longingly, he saw his wife walking through the coffee trees. She had her long hair hanging loose down her back, and her wet hair dampened the back of her red dress. Slippery Ochro wondered why she was wearing her best dress, which was reserved for special occasions. When she was near, Slippery Ochro asked her, "You wear your new dress?"

"Yes. The new dress hang up there. When I gon wear it? When I dead? I feel so glad that you ask Mohabir to let we build we house here. We don't got to pay rent. You talk to him already?"

"This is weird. I been also thinking how lucky we be that Mohabir allow us to build our house on he s land. We married for too long. Mohabir gon come down in a few minutes. He gon ask Dularie to join us."

Meanwhile, when Slippery Ochro left him, Mohabir went in the bedroom, and saw Dularie sitting up, having been unable to go back to sleep after being awakened by the knocking on the door. She was hanging her head, and rubbing her eyes, apparently anxious to go back to sleep.

"That was Slippery Ochro," Mohabir told her. "He bring the bottle of Russian Bear he won, and he want we to take a drink with him." He sat at the edge of the bed, and waited apprehensively for Dularie's response.

Dularie's two brothers were alcoholics, and she always wondered why they couldn't have just one or two drinks and then stop, like she and Mohabir did for years. After drinking too much the previous night, and drinking again at lunch, she did not want to tell Mohabir that she badly wanted another drink. She and Mohabir would have perhaps taken one or two drinks before dinner, but she was not averse to being persuaded to start drinking at that time.

"All right!" Then she added as an afterthought, "Once they don't make it a habit." She got up to change her dress.

Mohabir was relieved—he also wanted a drink. As he selected his best *house* khaki trousers and a blue shirt, he thought about Phulmattie, and hoped that she would not do or say anything to reveal what happened between them.

Mohabir and Dularie went to the kitchen where Mohabir took four glasses, while Dularie grabbed a bottle of Coke to be used as chaser, both acting as if they were reluctant, but inwardly happy that they were about to get the *hair of the dog*. When they went to the bottom house, Mohabir tried to hide his displeasure when he saw Slippery Ochro sitting in his favorite chair, and remained standing for a while, hoping that Slippery Ochro would get up and take another chair. When Slippery Ochro did not move, Mohabir was about to tell him to sit in another chair, but he was appeased when he noticed Phulmattie smiling at him with all her gold toothed splendor, and sat in another chair, after handing each person a glass.

"You take the maiden," Slippery Ochro told Mohabir as he handed him the bottle.

Dularie was embarrassed by Slippery Ochro's ribald language and her blood rushed to her face as she looked down, but Phulmattie chuckled as Mohabir took the bottle of Russian Bear, broke the seal, and threw a little bit of rum on the ground, which was daubed with a clay and cow-dung mix. Then he poured tall drinks for Dularie and himself before passing the bottle to Slippery Ochro, who poured for himself and Phulmattie. Slippery Ochro did not seem to mind that Phulmattie's eyes were glued to Mohabir, but Dularie kept looking at Phulmattie and Mohabir, confused about what was going on around her. Mohabir, on the other hand, avoided looking at Phulmattie, except for quick, furtive glances.

"So Gobin building an extension on his house," Slippery Ochro informed Mohabir as they raised their glasses for their first drink. "He got a big house already. I don't know why he want a bigger house. Two of his children marry and move out already, and Data is their last child. She already engage, and gon get married soon."

"He want show off," Phulmattie said. "He got lil[34] money and how he gon let people know that he dey[35] good? How many new shirt and pants he gon wear? So he gon build his house bigger to show people. We happy in the small house you allow us to build."

Always showing support for his wife, Slippery Ochro reached for the bottle. "Let he build his big house. You know I help him half a day and he buy only one bottle of rum? I don't want payment, but a small piece woulda help. He know I don't work. Mohabir and Dularie got money, but look how nice they sit down with us and drink."

Slippery Ochro took the liberty of pouring drinks and chasers for everybody, before raising his glass in a silent toast.

Mohabir and his wife were already feeling the buzz from the first drink. As they raised their glasses for the next one, both knew they were being manipulated, but also aware that they enjoyed the attention that Slippery Ochro and Phulmattie lavished on them, each of them also thinking that they could do nothing about the situation in which they found themselves.

What they were not aware of was that they could, in fact do something, and ask Slippery Ochro and Phulmattie to leave, but they were so kind and empathetic that they did not even entertain that thought. Indeed, an unbiased observer would have labelled Mohabir and Dularie as people pleasers.

As Mohabir put down his glass after the second drink, he glanced at Phulmattie, and saw her staring at him with her gold-toothed smile. He began to feel very self-conscious and resolved not to meet her eyes for the remainder of the night.

At one point, the dogs started barking as they did when someone was visiting, and Mohabir got up and went outside the circle of light to see who it was. He was surprised to see Gobin, dressed in an immaculately ironed black serge trousers, blue long-sleeved shirt, and flourishing a bottle of Russian Bear in his left hand.

---

[34] Small amount
[35] Everything is okay with him

Gobin greeted him. "Mohabir, I come to have a drink with you and Slippery Ochro."

Mohabir led him to join the others, and as soon as they entered the circle of light, Gobin addressed Slippery Ochro. "Slippery Ochro, I was passing to go to your house, and I see the light and you and Mohabir drinking, so I come in. I sorry that I had to leave you today. I had to go and talk to the contractor."

"I so glad to see you. I was telling Mohabir how kind you are. And how you house gon look nice with the extension. If you need any more help building, let me know. Mohabir, you gon get a glass for Gobin?"

Mohabir was slightly annoyed at being ordered about in his own house, but did not know how to object without making a scene. As a small act of defiance, he turned to Phulmattie, and told her, "You know where Dularie and I keep the glasses. Go and get a glass for Gobin."

Flashing her gold teeth, Phulmattie left for the kitchen.

Dularie, who had been quiet for most of the evening, was deeply disturbed by the verbal exchanges. *Slippery Ochro order Mohabir as if he own the house. And Mohabir ask Phulmattie to get the glass for Gobin as if she is his wife. I am his wife.* "I gon get the glass," she told Mohabir.

By then Phulmattie was at the foot of the stairs. Instead of returning to her seat, she waited for Dularie and accompanied her to the kitchen.

"Gobin got plenty money," Phulmattie told her. "Like he don't know what to do with his money. Why he putting extension on his house? Is only he and Ellen." She waited a while, and getting no response from Dularie, continued, "Where he getting all the money from? He got his farm, but how much money the farm gon bring?"

Dularie thought: *Why she concerned about other people for? Mohabir and I don't care about how much money people got. Or how big they making their house. We satisfy with what we got. Before Slippery Ochro and Phulmattie build they house on we land, we live quiet and easy. Mohabir give me one or two drink and we eat. Now like our house become a rum shop. And Phulmattie want me to worry about other people. I don't care how rich other people be. Once Mohabir and me okay, I feel nice.*

Then she realized that Phulmattie expected her to say something. "Well, he bring a bottle of rum for everybody. Leh we take this glass for him."

"All right! At least he buy a bottle of rum. But I still want to know where he get all the money from."

The two women walked down the stairs, with Dularie holding the glass. When they reached the bottom-house, Phulmattie grabbed the glass from Dularie, and flashing her gold teeth at Gobin, she handed him the glass. "I bring a glass for you," she said sweetly.

Mohabir noticed that she kept her hand on the glass for just a bit longer than was necessary, her fingers pressed against Gobin's. He was perplexed, but rationalized that Phulmattie probably had too much to drink. Then he glanced at Dularie, who sat on her chair uncomfortably observing everything going on around her.

When the five people finished the first bottle of rum, and also finished the bottle that Gobin brought. Gobin pulled out a five-dollar bill from his pocket and handed it to Slippery Ochro. "I too tired to go to Prashad to buy another bottle. Who gon go?"

Mohabir was bored of sitting down for so long, and he took the money from Gobin's hand, asserting, "I got to stretch me legs. I gon l go."

In spite of Phulmattie holding Gobin's fingers, Mohabir felt appreciated when, grabbing the flashlight from the table, Phulmattie also got up. "I gon go with you. It dark, and I don't want you to step in a hole and fall down and break your face." Then she laughed and added, "And if you break the bottle of rum, what we gon do?"

Dularie was confused and remained silent, but appeared far from happy, as Mohabir and Phulmattie walked away from the circle of light, with Phulmattie leading the way with the flashlight. Slippery Ochro appeared quite nonplussed with the situation, and sat in Mohabir's rocking chair, observing Gobin and Dularie with an enigmatic smile.

Gobin, who was much more worldly than Mohabir, was aware of Slippery Ochro's and Phulmattie's antics, and knew that Mohabir and Dularie were being played. He looked at Dularie reflectively, and thought, *They lived such a peaceful and upright life. I know that their lives will become interesting in a bad way, but I don't know how.*

Phulmattie slowed down to allow Mohabir to catch up with her, and they walked quite close together, the focused light from the flashlight illuminating their way. "I scared of labaria," she told Mohabir as she moved even closer to him.

The rum he had consumed made Mohabir careless and adventurous, and he put his arm around Phulmattie's shoulders. "Don't be afraid. Keep the flashlight in front and look carefully. Plenty people walk here and labaria didn't bite them. But my snake is beginning to awake."

Phulmattie ran her arms quickly along his crotch, "Tell your snake to go to sleep till we ready," she told him as she emitted a ribald laugh.

They entered Prashad's rum shop, where they bought a bottle of Russian Bear rum and four Pepsis. "Where are the empty bottles?" Prashad asked them.

"I forget them at home. I gon bring them tomorrow."

"All right Mohabir. I won't charge you any deposit for the bottles. You know that bottles scarce. The Pepsi bottler buying Coca Cola bottles and destroying them, and the Coca Cola bottler buying Pepsi bottles and destroying them. They want to destroy each other business. They have to get new bottles from the States, and that is expensive. Bring back the empties in the morning, because the Pepsi truck coming tomorrow."

"Okay! I got some Coca Cola bottles. You want me to bring them, or destroy them."

Prashad laughed. "Bring them too. Coca Cola bottler is Indian. Pepsi bottler is *Potagee*.[36] You want the Indian man business fail, and the Potagee man to get rich?"

In his puckish mood, Mohabir responded, "Okay! I gon break the Pepsi bottle and bring the Coca Cola bottle."

Prashad knew that Mohabir was teasing, and chuckled. "Break what you want, and bring what you want. Next time I gon charge you rass deposit." Then he decided to do some teasing of his own. "So, what happen? It look as if you take a second wife?" And he looked at Phulmattie.

Phulmattie rested her hand lightly on Mohabir's arm and spoke for the first time since they entered the rum shop. "You think Mohabir like you, arguing about a ten-cent deposit on bottles? He allow Slippery Ochro and me to build we house on his land, and he don't charge we rent."

Prashad knew better than to pick an argument with Phulmattie, and remained silent as Phulmattie and Mohabir turned to leave.

As they approached the door, Phulmattie turned around for one parting shot. "You sure you didn't water down this rum?" she asked Prashad.

---

[36] Portuguese

- 44 -

"The bottle seal. How I gon water it down?"

"You can open it, water it down, and then seal it again."

Prashad wanted to tell her not to come to his shop if she believed that he was watering down the rum, but he was very much aware that Phulmattie and Slippery Ochro constituted a lethal force, and he was afraid. He regretted his jibe about Mohabir taking a second wife.

"The rum good," was all he could say as Phulmattie and Mohabir disappeared into the night.

"I gon fix he up good," Phulmattie told Mohabir as soon as they moved out of earshot. "I won't let anybody take they eyes pass you when I around," she continued as she moved closer to him and rested her hand gently on his arm.

Mohabir always had a good relationship with Prashad, and felt very uncomfortable about the interaction that had just passed. He and Prashad had indulged in good-natured teasing for as long as he could remember, and neither had harbored any hard feelings. He silently prayed that Phulmattie would not cause any trouble.

I hope that Phulmattie forget the whole thing, he said to himself.

As they neared home, Phulmattie moved a little farther from Mohabir as they entered his yard.

Mohabir's hopes were dashed. As soon as they went into the bottom house, Phulmattie told her husband, "Prashad mek me feel cheap. He tell Mohabir that that it look as if he tek a second wife when he see me wid him. Leh we fix he up good."

Slippery Ochro was incensed and turned to Mohabir. "I poor, but I don't take any rass pass from anybody. Because Prashad got some money, he think that he can tell anybody anything. I gon sue his backside."

"Prashad was just joking. Prashad and me always joke with each other," Mohabir told Slippery Ochro in an attempt to soothe him.

Slippery Ochro would not be appeased. "Shakespeare said, *Many a true thing pass as joke.* Prashad make a joke, but people gon think that it true."

Nobody in the group questioned whether Shakespeare did say what Slippery Ochro attributed to him, because everybody recognized that the great writer was White, was English, and that he said many wise things. He was most likely to say a wise thing like that.

"I know that you gon represent me, and you won't take it lying down," Phulmattie told her husband.

Encouraged, Slippery Ochro turned to Mohabir, "You are a witness to how Prashad insult me. Prashad know that Phulmattie is me wife, and for him to tell you that you take her for a second wife is an insult to me. He think he got money, I gon sue he rass for some of he money. Gobin and Dularie, you are witness that Mohabir and Phulmattie just go to buy a bottle of rum because we run out, and then Prashad start spreading all kind of rumor. Soon, the whole of Canal gon talk about Phulmattie and Mohabir, because Prashad start his stupidness. How I gon hold up me head in Canal now? I gon go see Haynes in town tomorrow. He handle these cases without any payment, and he take a percentage of the money when his clients win. Prashad don't know who he playing with."

In an attempt to defuse the situation, Gobin told everybody, "The bottle rum winking at us." Then he opened it, threw a few drops on the ground, and poured for everybody. He had hoped that the fire which was just lit would be quenched, but was disappointed.

Before she drank, Phulmattie told her husband, "I gon go with you to Georgetown. I try to be a nice person, but Prashad take his eyes pass me. I glad that you represent me."

She turned to Dularie, "Dularie girl, you got to stand up for me. You see that all I done was accompany Mohabir to buy a bottle of rum, and Prashad start spreading all kind of rumor. Mohabir is yuh husband, and you gon get bad name too. You can't stay quiet all your life and let people who got money take advantage of you."

Dularie didn't know how to respond. All her life she had tried to live peacefully with all the villagers, and even with people who lived outside the village. When she got married and came to her husband's village, Prashad and his wife were one of the first people she met, and she bought all her groceries from them. She would take credit from Prashad during the week and pay her account in full every Saturday when Mohabir got paid. Their mutual, unspoken respect lasted all these years, and she did not want to spoil it now. She desperately wanted to make peace, and entreated Phulmattie, "Phulmattie, Prashad was just teasing Mohabir and you. He didn't mean anything."

Phulmattie was incensed. "He didn't mean anything? When the whole of Canal start talking, he gon tell them that he didn't mean anything? He don't know who he playing with. Me husband is a quiet, quiet man, but he don't take no shit from nobody. Prashad don't know who he messing with. Shakespeare also say, *Goat na know the size of he BT til he swallow genip seed.*

This genip seed gon stick in he rass. Prashad gon find out the trouble he cause. Dularie, we ah woman together. We cannot let people spoil our character. The next thing they gon want to do is *juk*[37] out we eye."

"But Prashad just joking," Dularie said weakly.

"Just joking! If anybody tell you that somebody husband take you for he second wife, how you gon like it?"

Dularie wanted to tell Phulmattie that she would not act in such a manner that people would have cause to make such a comment, but she was scared of Phulmattie. She realized that she was also scared of Slippery Ochro, and thought *What pugatory we put ourself in?* She was jolted into the present by a nudge from Phulmattie.

"If somebody tell you that Slippery Ochro take you for his second wife, you gon like it?"

In her wildest imagination, Dularie could not see herself as Slippery Ochro's wife, much less his second wife and responded with a simple, "No!"

This was the encouragement Phulmattie wanted. "Well, I don't like it either. Because we poor, people think that they can take advantage of we." Then she called forth her arsenal of tears. Between sobs, she turned to Slippery Ochro. "We gon see Haynes tomorrow?"

"Yes. We better stop drinking now." Then he looked at the half full bottle and reconsidered. "Well, we can take one or two more, and then stop. We gon try and get a car for the nine o'clock boat and reach Georgetown at about ten. Then we can see Haynes." With that, Slippery Ochro poured a round of heavy drinks for everyone, along with the Pepsi as chasers.

Mohabir and Gobin were mesmerized, and realized that they were involved in something they wanted no part of, and that they could not do anything to stop it.

When the bottle was drained, Slippery Ochro and Phulmattie went to their house, leaving Gobin and Mohabir racking their brains to find an escape out of the net which was cast around them.

Gobin asked Mohabir, "What we gon do?"

Even in her drunken state, Dularie was very much aware of her husband's discomfort when he started to vigorously scratch his head with

---

[37] Poke

both hands. He hadn't cut his fingernails for some time, and Dularie knew that she would have to apply coconut oil on his scalp for about a week in order for the lacerations to heal.

Gobin waited until Mohabir stopped scratching, and rephrased his question. "We gon let Slippery Ochro and his wife tell us what to do?"

"No! Prashad and me were friends since we were small. I can't take him to court now. The man was just joking. Let Slippery Ochro and Phulmattie do what they like. I na gon take Prashad to court."

Gobin corrected Mohabir. "You not taking Prashad to court. Slippery Ochro and his wife taking Prashad to court. You just a witness."

Mohabir scratched his head briefly before making a formal announcement. "I will not go to court to give witness."

Gobin, who was a bit more worldly than Mohabir, enlightened him. "They will give you a summons, and command you to appear. Then you have to go, or else they will give you a fine or send you to jail."

Mohabir, sobered up immediately. He never imagined himself or any of his relatives going to jail. "Then I gon go to court and say that Prashad never told me that it look like I take a second wife."

"They will make you swear on the bible."

"But I don't believe in the bible. I believe in the Ramayan[38]."

"Even if they make you swear on a comic book, you still have to tell the truth, or they can charge you with perjury."

Gobin saw the blank look on Mohabir's face, and elaborated. "Perjury is when you tell a lie in court after you swear to tell the truth. The judge can sentence you to jail for it."

In his wildest imagination, Mohabir could not imagine himself being in jail, and when he heard the word *jail* mentioned in reference to himself, he was traumatized. Accustomed to his rustic life, he was thoroughly confused. "You mean that even if I don't want to be involved in Slippery Ochro story, they can force me to be involved? If I don't want to swear on the bible, they can make me? You mean if I don't want to put my friend in trouble, they can force me to put him in trouble?"

"Not wanting to swear on the bible, they can fix. I remember reading an article in the *Daily Graphic*. Looku was representing a man who refuse to

---

[38] Hindu holy book

swear on the bible, and the judge postpone the case and they got a Koran for him to swear on. He refuse to swear on the Koran, because he said that he believed that it was a holy book for prayers, and not for swearing. They made him raise his right hand swear to tell the truth in a court of law. You can't escape, Mohabir."

Mohabir scratched his head vigorously, and when he removed his hand from his head, Dularie could see blood under his fingernails. "What we gon do?" he asked Gobin, almost pleadingly.

"Everything happen too quickly. Leh we go to sleep now, and in the morning we gon think about it. When I drink, I like to have a nice time. I don't like to think about problems."

"Me too!" Mohabir said. "I drink because I want to feel good, not to pick quarrels, or create problems. Dularie and me want to live our life quiet and easy."

Then he glanced at Dularie to discover that she was slumped on her chair, drool hanging from the side of her open mouth. Mohabir was embarrassed, and looked at Gobin, who was looking in the direction of Slippery Ochro's house, and pretending not to notice Dularie.

"I gon go home now," Gobin told Mohabir, as he got up, and looked squarely at Mohabir, in a desperate attempt to save the faces of Mohabir and Dularie. He had known Mohabir since childhood and had welcomed Dularie when she came to Canal as Mohabir's bride. Eventually, Dularie had earned the reputation of being one of the most respected and upright women in the village.

It only one time, Gobin said to himself. *I will not tell anybody, and she will still maintain the respect of everybody.* Then he reflected on the situation and had to admit, *But with Slippery Ochro and Phulmattie living on their land, I know that it will not be one time.*

As he turned to go home, he thought, *All I came for was one drink, and look what trouble I find myself in. I got so many things to do. I don't have time to spend on court cases. Slippery Ochro likes court cases. He should be a lawyer, and then he can spend every day in court, and get paid for it. And Phulmattie is the same. My wife told me not to ask Slippery Ochro to help me to haul the timber. Is me hard-ears got me here.*

**

When Gobin went home, Sumintra, his wife, was lying in the hammock inside their house. He sat on a chair beside the hammock, and recounted the events of the evening to her.

Sumintra, a buxom, voluptuous woman, who had her hair cut and permed by a hairstylist in Georgetown, sat up and looked intensely at her husband. "You know how Slippery Ochro and Phulmattie staan,. Now look what happen. You want to waste yuh time in court?"

"I gon try and not get involved," he said weakly.

"You already involved. You know Slippery Ochro and Phulmattie only look for court case. Remember when they take Khrisna to court because Phulmattie say that his latrine smell and they could not sleep at night. And that cause them to get sick?"

Gobin laughed. "I remember! The magistrate throw out the case, because Khrisna lawyer argue that he had no control over how his latrine smell."

"But look at the time Khrisna had to spend to go to court. And he had to hire a lawyer."

"Slippery Ochro not taking me to court. He taking Prashad to court."

"Prashad and you friends for years. You gon go as witness against him."

"If I get summons, I got to go. But they won't summon me. I wasn't there with Mohabir and Phulmattie. I hear only what Phulmattie say when she come back from Prashad rum shop."

Sumintra could only put her hands upon her head and exclaim, "God, what *janghat*[39] you put pon we head now?" She began to close the doors and windows in preparation for their bedtime, knowing that their sleep would be fitful that night.

---

[39] Trouble

Chapter 5

"All conflict can be traced back to someone's feelings getting hurt, don't you think?"

—Liane Moriarty—

Big Little Lies

Mohabir was having trouble waking Dularie. He did not want anybody passing on the road to see his wife in this condition, so he had extinguished the lamp, leaving the glasses and bottles to be cleared up in the morning.

"Slippery Ochro and Phulmattie make you drink so much," he told her as he put her arm over his shoulder, and holding her by the waist, half carried her up the stairs and into the bedroom.

She fell asleep with her house clothes on, and Mohabir, intoxicated, and feeling exhausted after bringing Dularie to bed, also fell asleep without changing into his pajamas.

He was awakened by Dularie's retching and vomiting, which was not totally unexpected. For two nights in a row his wife, who had never had more than one or two drinks, had drunk to the point where she was vomiting.

What happen with us? he thought. Then he remembered Prashad, and how Slippery Ochro promised to take him to court. *That man and his wife brought nothing but trouble since they build their house on our land.* As he thought of Phulmattie, he felt himself getting an erection, and as he got harder, his thoughts softened, not only towards her, but also towards Slippery Ochro, because they came together as a package. *Life is like this. Prashad should not have made the joke about me taking a second wife, with Phulmattie present.* He raised himself on his elbow and found himself thinking of Phulmattie as he rubbed Dularie's back. "I gon go and get some water for you," he told her.

Dularie was able to stop vomiting long enough to retort, "You gon bring it alone, or Phulmattie gon bring it with you?"

Mohabir was aghast. He was convinced that Dularie had no inkling about what was happening between him and Phulmattie, but realized that he had not factored in a woman's intuition. "What you mean?"

"You think I don't see how that woman looking at you? She look at you more than she look at she own husband. Since I marry you, I never look at another man, and look how you and she acting."

Mohabir was relieved when she started retching again—this prevented her from chastising him further. He brought a cup of water and a basin from the kitchen. As he put the basin beside Dularie, he thought that it was a waste of time, because she would have to clean the floor anyway. He gave her the cup of water to rinse her mouth and resumed rubbing her back until she stopped vomiting and fell asleep.

He continued sitting on his side of the bed and reflected on what was happening in their lives since Slippery Ochro's and Phulmattie's lives became intertwined with theirs. *We were too weak to tell them that we wouldn't allow them to build their house on our land. We allow them to encourage us to drink almost every night, and look what happen with me and Phulmattie.*

Unable to go back to sleep, Mohabir got up and glanced at his wife, with whom he had a loving relationship for so long. *I gon put a stop to this stupidness*, he told himself, as he quietly returned to the kitchen to grab his pipe, tobacco and matches. Opening the door quietly, he went to the verandah and lit his pipe. Leaning back, he enjoyed looking at the sky. The moon had come out and the stars were twinkling in full splendor. Mohabir looked around his property, and admired the outline of the trees. *To a stranger, they must look like bush*, he thought. *But they are all fruit trees.* His eyes moved from the mango tree towering over the coffee trees, to the chestnut tree, the cashew tree, and the star-apple tree. Then he looked at the spot where Slippery Ochro had built his house, and thought, *I try to help him out, but look what happen.*

Hearing a click as the door to the verandah opened, Mohabir turned to see his wife.

"I hear when you come out of the room. When you didn't come back to bed, I know that you come out here for a smoke." She was one of the few women who liked the smell of the tobacco smoke, and Mohabir enjoyed her company, along with his pipe, except when he was playing checkers. They sat together in silence, lost in their thoughts, although each of them knew that the other was also thinking of Slippery Ochro and Phulmattie, and the impact they were having on their lives. After a while, Dularie said, "So Slippery Ochro and Phulmattie going to town to sue Prashad?"

Remembering what Dularie told him earlier, Mohabir was instantly on the alert, and took a few minutes before answering. "Slippery Ochro just looking for an excuse to take somebody to court."

If he thought that he would get off easily, he was wrong.

"But why Prashad say that it look like you take Phulmattie for a second wife?"

"Prashad always making jokes. He was just teasing me because Phulmattie go with me to buy the bottle of rum."

Phulmattie's accompanying Mohabir to Prashad had been bothering Dularie, and she was happy that the matter came up. "Why she had to go with you? First, she go with you to weed the coffee walk. Then she go with you in the night to buy rum. Prashad right to tell you that it look like you take a second wife. She act like she is your second wife. She bare face."

Since he was not asked a question, Mohabir decided that it was wise to keep quiet, not realizing that sometimes silence meant an acceptance of guilt.

The silence of quite a few minutes was broken by Dularie. "What happen? You're not saying anything?"

"Slippery Ochro say that she could go with me to weed the coffee walk, and he been there when she go with me to Prashad," was all he could say.

"I been there too, but it don't mean that I agree with it. Slippery Ochro and his wife using you. You are a respectable man in Canal, and they think that if you close to them, people gon respect them. They don't know that people laughing at them behind their back. Slippery Ochro don't like work. He like to take advantage of people like we, and Phulmattie flaunting she self before men so that they cannot think clearly."

Again, Mohabir decided not to say anything, because he was afraid that he might incriminate himself.

Dularie asked, "You going to give witness against Prashad?"

Mohabir felt obliged to answer this direct question. "If Slippery Ochro and Phulmattie take the matter to court, and they call me as a witness, I got to go. But I gon say that Prashad been just joking. Then let the lawyers fight between themself."

Chapter 6

"If there is someone in your life that you can't speak the truth to, and you walk on eggshells to avoid upsetting them, you are being controlled or manipulated!

—Unknown—

Although Mohabir and Dularie could not yet see the sun, it was beginning to get brighter, and they both realized that they had been bickering until dawn. Without articulating it, both agreed that it was useless to go back to bed, and they made their way into the kitchen to prepare breakfast. Dularie started kneading the flour for the roti while Mohabir cut the boulangers in small pieces, before peeling some potatoes. They had been following this ritual for years, and there was little need for communication as they went about their specific tasks. Mohabir had already lit the fireside and put water to boil for coffee. Husband and wife took solace in this comfortable routine, after the turmoil of the last few days.

"You know, Dularie, I been thinking—"

Dularie never got to know what her husband was thinking because there was a loud knock on the door. When Mohabir went to answer, there was Phulmattie, wearing a red, flowered dress and a pair of black shoes. She had a gold necklace which she wore outside her dress for it to be more conspicuous.

The sun was already out by then, and reflected on the necklace and Phulmattie's gold teeth as she smiled widely in greeting. "I come to ask Dularie if I can borrow she brown handbag. You know Slippery Ochro and me going to town, and I need a handbag to put me things in."

Mohabir scratched his head vigorously, and was quiet for a few seconds. He was relieved to hear Dularie's footsteps behind him. Dularie held her hands upright in front of her, because they were smeared with flour, and she didn't want any to drip on the floor.

Without waiting for Dularie to greet her Phulmattie repeated her request, "Dularie, gal, I got to go to town with Slippery Ochro, and I need a handbag to put in my pressure pills, my kerchief and some other things. I notice a brown handbag on your kitchen cabinet. If you lend me for today, I gon give you back when I come back from town. You want anything from town?"

Mohabir made a weak attempt to protect his wife. "You got some things in your bag. Right, Dularie?"

"Gal, if you can take your things out and lend me the bag, just for today. I got to take my pills at twelve o'clock. If I lose them and I don't take them, I gon faint away. Look at how Sahadeo get a stroke because he didn't take his pressure tablet."

Dularie was determined that she would not be the cause of Phulmattie getting a stroke because she had refused to lend her the handbag. "All right! Wait until I wash my hands and take my things out of my handbag." She promptly went to the kitchen, washed the flour off her hands, emptied her handbag, and returned to the verandah, where Mohabir stood awkwardly with Phulmattie.

"You sure you don't want anything from Georgetown?" Phulmattie asked Dularie as the bag changed hands.

"No, Phulmattie! I got everything I need," Dularie replied, as she rested her hand on her husband's arm.

Phulmattie smiled widely as she accepted the handbag, hurried down the stairs, and made her way to her house.

When she disappeared among the coffee trees, Mohabir turned to Dularie and said in a voice that was not unkind, "You too soft. You should'a tell her that you got things in the bag that you don't want to take out."

"And when she dead, or she get a stroke because she didn't take her pills, I gon make her well again?"

"You too soft," Mohabir repeated.

"You soft too. That's why all kind of people take advantage of we. I don't want to bring back long-time story, but remember when we get married? Your brother take all of our presents, including money, to his wife's brother's place, and we get only some of the wedding presents. Only God knows how much money they take. I see how many presents we receive, because my wedding was the first one which my parents had, and they give wedding presents to so many people. People who come to our wedding feel that they had to return my parents' generosity. I was surprised when I see how few presents we receive after I see so many in the *maroo*.[40]"

Mohabir replied, "You know my brother and his wife really remind me of Slippery Ochro and Phulmattie. They all encourage each other to use people and take advantage of them. I did not even think of the presents until I saw how few we received. What good the presents do them? We not short of anything."

Dularie decided to capitalize on Mohabir's statement. "You right! We not short of anything. Let Phulmattie use the handbag and she can give me back when she come home from Georgetown. The handbag na gon spoil."

Mohabir, decided to give his two cents' worth. "The handbag na gon spoil, but they going to town to make trouble for me and Prashad. And she borrow your handbag to do it. It like somebody ask you to lend him your cutlass so that he can chop you up."

"What you want me to do? Just tell her *No*?"

When Mohabir started to scratch his head, Dularie knew that they were heading for a heated argument, and she relented, "Let she go and see which lawyer she want. All them lawyers are liars anyway. She gon bring back the handbag, and we gon deal with what Prashad tell you. You fry up the boulanger and potato and I gon cook the roti. Leh we enjoy our breakfast, and let Slippery Ochro and Phulmattie sing and dance to their own music."

She glanced at Mohabir and noticed that the head scratching had eased up, as he went to the sink, washed his hands, and started to peel the potatoes.

Dularie kneaded the flour, rolled it into a lump and then pinched out chunks which she molded into balls. She would then use the *bellnah*[41] to flatten the balls before putting them on the *tawa*[42] to cook. When they were finished cooking the roti and frying the potatoes and boulangers, Dularie dished them out in plates, and smiled when she remembered Mohabir's frequent flatteries that the food always tasted sweeter when she dished it out. Then they sat the table, and looked at each other, the steaming coffee and the food remaining untouched.

---

[40] A decorated area in which the marriage ceremony takes place.
[41] Rolling pin
[42] A flat iron on which roti is cooked

Finally, Mohabir said, "We drink too much last night. I hungry, but I don't feel like eating." He looked at Dularie, hoping for a response, but she just sat there not touching her food or coffee, without saying anything.

"I think a small drink gon open our appetite," he continued.

Dularie felt the same way, but did not consider the drinking option, because it was unthinkable for her to take a drink before breakfast. She had never done so in her life. However, considering the appetizing breakfast before her, and the fact that she was hungry, but with an upset stomach, the idea appealed to her.

"But don't make it a habit," he teased, anticipating her own words, as he got up and went to the cupboard to retrieve the bottle of five-year-old El Dorado which he had reserved for him and Dularie. "This gon make us enjoy our breakfast."

Mohabir poured liberal amounts of rum and Pepsi in two glasses, and saw Dularie making a face after the first sip. "It taste like piss after last night, don't it? After one or two sips, it gon taste better," he predicted.

Despite her upset stomach, Dularie took two gulps of the El Dorado, and sure enough, she began to feel a warm glow in her stomach. She finished the glass quite easily, and sat looking at Mohabir who had also finished his drink and was looking around the kitchen as if he was trying to make up his mind about something.

Dularie decided for him. "I know that you want another drink. Mix another one for me too." She slid her glass towards him.

A wide smile appeared on Mohabir's face as he sprang up with alacrity, made his way to the cabinet and returned with the bottle of El Dorado. When he poured two large drinks for himself and his wife, he raised the bottle to eye level, and announced, "This bottle punishing. There is just a little left at the bottom. Leh we finish it." He drained the bottle in the two glasses and squeezed it. "Just to make sure that we get all out," he told Dularie, laughing at his own joke.

"The five-year-old finish. You gon go with Phulmattie to buy another one?" Dularie teased Mohabir.

Mohabir recognized the tone of levity. "You mean my second wife?" he quipped.

"Many a true thing pass as joke," Dularie reminded him as they began to enjoy their breakfast.

The lightening of their mood lasted until two in the afternoon. Mohabir did not go to work in the farm because of the drinks he had consumed the previous evening and in the morning and, because he and Dularie retired to their bedroom after drinks and breakfast. This was something that they did when they were recently married, but now it was rare for them to make love so early in the morning, and they thoroughly enjoyed being together. Aided by the drinks that they had consumed, they both fell asleep, locked in each other's arms.

Dularie woke up briefly and looked at her husband, sleeping peacefully, and thought, *At our age, this is how life should be. We too old to get involved in other people business. I can sleep like this until dinner.* Mohabir started snoring and she threw her arms around him in a tighter embrace and drifted off to sleep again.

**

They were awakened by a loud knocking at the door. At first, both ignored it and continued napping. But the knocking got louder, and Mohabir raised himself up on his elbows and looked at Dularie, who was already awake.

"It Slippery Ochro or Phulmattie," he told her. "What we gon do?"

"Leave them. They gon go away." She hugged her husband and closed her eyes, although she knew that neither she nor her husband would go back to sleep.

The knocking continued, and they could hear Slippery Ochro shouting. "Mohabir, Dularie, WAKE UP! You not young anymore. We got some good news to tell you." Both Mohabir and Dularie groaned and got up.

"They not going to leave us alone," Dularie told her husband. "You better go and see what they want." Then she naively added, "Then you can come back to bed."

Mohabir put on his pants and shirt and went to the door. He was greeted by Slippery Ochro and Phulmattie. Both of them were smiling widely, and Slippery Ochro, dressed in his best blue serge trousers, and a clean white shirt, was waving a bottle of Russian Bear rum in his hand. Phulmattie was wearing a blue and rose dress, with her gold necklace prominently displayed.

Slippery Ochro said, "Haynes gon take our case. And we don't have to give him any money. He gon take his payment from the settlement money we gon get. I feel so glad, that I stop at Manbahal rum shop and buy a bottle. I not going to Prashad anymore. Besides, I think that he watering his rum. When I win this case, I gon take his ass to court for watering his rum."

Mohabir scratched his head furiously, and looked around for succor, which did arrive, in the form of Dularie, who had put on her dress and joined them by the door.

Phulmattie flashed her gold teeth triumphantly, "Dularie girl, you got life good, sleeping whenever you want. You hear what Slippery Ochro tell Mohabir! Haynes gon take our case. I don't like to drink so early. I know you don't like to drink so early too. But Slippery Ochro and me feel so happy that we buy a bottle and say that we gon take a lil drink. If it wasn't for you and Mohabir, we wouldn't a taken Prashad to court. We got you two to thank for it. I bring back yuh bag. I don't like to return things empty, so I put some walnut inside for you."

Both Dularie and Mohabir were perplexed. They knew that they didn't encourage Slippery Ochro and Phulmattie to take Prashad to court, and there was Phulmattie thanking them for it.

Soon they gon tell the whole of Canal that we encourage them to take Prashad to court, Mohabir thought. *I better put a stop to this.* "But we didn't encourage you to take Prashad to court," he told Slippery Ochro.

Slippery Ochro responded immediately. "But you agree to give witness that Prashad tell you that it look like you take a second wife when he see Phulmattie with you. That all the support we need to sue his backside. Haynes say that we got a good case, and he gon file the papers. You and Dularie come to the bottom house and we gon take a drink to celebrate."

"I gon say that Prashad was just joking. We always make joke with each other."

Slippery Ochro repeated, "Come take a drink with we at the bottom house."

Mohabir and Dularie looked at each other. Again, they were being invited to their own house for a drink. They also did not know whether they were too weak, too naïve, too kind, or if they also wanted a drink, but they just nodded and went to the kitchen to get glasses and Pepsis, while Slippery Ochro and Phulmattie went downstairs to wait. When Mohabir came downstairs holding four glasses, he was angry, but not surprised to see Slippery Ochro sitting in his favorite rocking chair. His anger was abated when he saw Phulmattie sitting on a two-seater bench with an empty space beside her. He put the glasses on the table, sat beside Phulmattie and they all waited for Dularie to bring the Pepsi for the chasers. They heard Dularie walking down the stairs, and were surprised when she stopped on the second-to-last stair from the bottom.

Dularie looked at Slippery Ochro sitting on Mohabir's favorite chair, and then looked at Mohabir sitting near Phulmattie and thought, *They taking each other place. What happening in our house?*

Phulmattie smiled widely, and said, "Dularie girl, we glad that we can celebrate with you. People think that they can take their eyes pass us because we women. But these are *madam days*.[43] We got to stand up for ourselves. Me mother had to drink in the kitchen while the men sit at the table and drink openly. Those days done. We work harder than the men, but they don't appreciate us. Sit down, girl and let we take a drink. Prashad buying this drink for us, but he don't know it yet."

Mohabir's head started to itch, but he restrained himself. *This woman inviting Dularie to sit and have a drink in our own house. That is not her place.* But he did not know what to say aloud, so he got up and took the Pepsi from Dularie, intending to give his seat near Phulmattie to her. When he looked back at the two-seater bench, he saw that Phulmattie had spread herself so that she took over the whole bench, and Dularie had no choice but to sit in one of the other chairs. As soon as she was seated, Mohabir made a move to sit near her, but was interrupted by Phulmattie.

"Mohabir, your glass here. Come let me tell you what Haynes tell we."

Mohabir obediently went to sit near Phulmattie, who told him, "You know that Haynes got his office on Croal Street? When we go there, the office full of people, but we didn't have to wait long, because Haynes know us. You know that he handle our case when Chunilall threaten to chop Slippery Ochro up. After Chunilall tell Slippery Ochro that he gon chop him, every afternoon when he come home from work, Chunilall sit on his front step and sharpen his cutlass, so that Slippery Ochro could see. Slippery Ochro was so frighten that he could not eat or sleep." At this point, Phulmattie hesitated, sighed, and then dropped her voice slightly, "Or have sex," she added, giggling. "And he start to lose weight. Haynes win the case for us. Chunilall lucky that he didn't lose his house and land. But we get five hundred dollars from him. I don't think that he gon threaten anybody again. Now we gon see what gon happen with Prashad case."

Slippery Ochro opened the bottle, and anxiously looked under the cap for a picture of a Russian bear. When Mohabir saw him twist his mouth,

---

[43] Modern days

he surmised that the Russian bear had eluded Slippery Ochro, who overcame his disappointment and started pouring drinks for everybody.

Phulmattie was the first to raise her glass. "Leh we hope that we win this case," she toasted.

Mohabir and Dularie hesitated because of their relationship with Prashad, and they never understood why they drank to that toast. But they did clink their glasses together, drank, and enjoyed the warm glow of the alcohol as it burned a way down their throats.

Slippery Ochro glanced at Mohabir, who was thinking about his relationship with Prashad, and the fact that he did not want to betray him. "Mohabir, don't worry. Haynes tell we that everything gon be all right. You know that he only take cases that he can win. I know that you and Dularie worried about us. Don't worry. We gon win this case."

Phulmattie moved a bit closer to Mohabir, and nudged him with her legs. Mohabir wanted to tell Slippery Ochro that he was not worried about his winning the case at all, but with Phulmattie's legs pressed against his, all he could say was, "We gon see what gon happen."

Slippery Ochro took this for a statement of support, and replied, "With your evidence, we gon win for sure."

Looking directly at Dularie, Phulmattie said, "We can't let any Tom, Dick and Harry take their rass pass us. We got to stand up for our rights. Right gal?"

There was a long pause, with everybody looking at Dularie for an answer. Dularie was not quick witted enough, nor smart enough to realize the implications of her answer. In addition, a deep-seated desire to please caused her to reply, "Right!"

The four continued drinking until the bottle was empty, and they sat looking at each other, until Mohabir felt uncomfortable. By then, the sun had already set, and the chickens were making their way to the coop. A few, made their way to their favorite roosts on the lower branches of the orange trees.

Mohabir felt that he could not have people in his house wanting another drink and not having it. Besides, although he had a drink or two frequently before dinner, whenever he had more than two drinks, he always felt a desire to have more. He suddenly remembered that he had put aside a bottle of rum under his bed,

"I got some more rum upstairs," he said, and walked up the stairs to get it.

There was a look of satisfaction on all the faces, including Dularie's, as he placed the bottle on the coffee table, and they resumed drinking. After the bottle was finished, Slippery Ochro and his wife contentedly made their way to their house, while Mohabir helped Dularie up the stairs for the second night in a row. After he led her to their bed and she lay down, Mohabir had the foresight to bring a basin and place it on the floor beside her before he went around to his side of the bed. They both slept in their house clothes.

Surprisingly, Dularie did not vomit during the night, but neither of them heard the cock crowing, or the birds chirping in the morning.

**

Later in the morning, Mohabir and Dularie were awake, but did not get up out of bed until they heard the knocking on the door. Simultaneously, they said, "Slippery Ochro," and looked at each other for a few minutes, trying to read each other's thoughts.

"I gon go and see what he want. You can rest some more," Mohabir said. When he opened the door, there was Phulmattie, still dressed in the long blue dress she slept in, and holding four ripe oranges in her hand. Mohabir could see the reflection of the oranges in her flashing gold teeth.

"Slippery Ochro say that after all the drink last night, you and Dularie gon need these. You just wake up, right? Dularie wake up yet?"

"Dularie still in bed," Mohabir replied.

"I gon peel these for the two of you, while you brush your teeth and so on."

Phulmattie did not wait for a reply, and Mohabir could feel her breasts as she brushed past him and made her way to the kitchen.

When Dularie came out of the bedroom, Phulmattie said, "Eh heh, Dularie girl, you lucky that you can sleep in late. Must be the drink we take last night. Slippery Ochro send over these oranges for you. I say that I gon peel them for you and Mohabir. Orange good for you when you drink."

It was on the tip of Dularie's tongue to ask Phulmattie where she got the oranges from, although she already knew the answer, but she was either too sluggish or too timid to ask, so she just sat down at the table, and looked at Mohabir, whose eyes were following Phulmattie's movements.

Phulmattie peeled the oranges, cut them in two, and put them in a plate on the table.

For a few seconds, Dularie felt pampered. When she was a little girl, her mother used to put treats in front of her like that, but she couldn't remember anybody doing that when she got older. She and Mohabir sucked the juice from the oranges.

Phulmattie lit the fireside and put water to boil for coffee. "You want me to knead the flour and cook some roti and bora for you?" she asked Dularie.

Oh my God! Dularie thought. She really nice. *It like having somebody working for you.* "Me head hurting, and I don't feel like eating anything, but I feel like drinking some coffee and taking some aspirin," she said.

"Where you keep the aspirin?"

"On the top shelf of the cabinet."

Phulmattie found the aspirin, opened the cap and took two to Dularie, along with a cup of water. "Drink it with water. As soon as the water boil, I gon make coffee for you and Mohabir. You know, it nice to drink your own coffee. You pick your coffee, you dry it, you mill it, and then you roast it and grind it yourself. It taste so nice. When you buy coffee, you don't know what they put inside. Some people mix the coffee with some of the skin from the coffee. I gon make enough for me and Slippery Ochro too. While the water hotting, I gon run over and call Slippery Ochro."

All Dularie's feelings of being pampered dissipated. All her plans of having a cup of coffee, and going back to bed were quashed. As they had done many times in the past, and would do many times in the future, she and her husband looked at each other, each wishing that the other would say something to rescue them from an undesirable situation.. Helplessly, they watched as Phulmattie hurried down the back stairs to get her husband.

Dularie looked at Mohabir sadly, and asked, "We gon start drinking again with Slippery Ochro and Phulmattie? I can't do this every day. And you didn't take your blood pressure medicine for two days now. What we gon do?"

"He just coming for coffee," Mohabir replied weakly.

"They must be run out of coffee," Dularie said hopefully, as she sucked the juice of the last bit of orange and put it in the plate. She got up to throw the rind out of the window.

Slippery Ochro and Phulmattie walked into the kitchen through the back door. Slippery Ochro was dressed in his work clothes, and had on a straw hat, which he took off as he entered the kitchen.

He was already dressed and been waiting for her, Dularie thought. *I wonder what they planning?*

The water was boiling by this time, and Phulmattie went straight to the fireside. "Where you keep the coffee?" she asked Dularie.

"In a Nestle container on the top left-hand shelf. The condense milk and the sugar on the same shelf too."

Phulmattie put the boiling water in a medium-sized pot, before adding four heaping spoons of coffee. She allowed the coffee to brew for a few minutes, before she strained it and then she added sugar and condensed milk. There was nothing odd about this, because almost everybody in Canal made coffee in this way for their families. The thought of making separate cups for everybody, and of catering for their individual preferences for drinking coffee did not exist. Phulmattie poured the coffee into four cups, and brought them to the table. As Dularie and Mohabir brought their steaming cups to their lips, they had a moment of feeling pampered until Phulmattie asked, "Where you keep the flour girl? I gon cook some roti for us. And I notice that you got some bora on the table. I gon fry it up before it spoil."

This woman taking over my kitchen, Dularie thought. But with her hangover, she was not up to objecting. Besides, she was not used to handling situations like these, and automatically answered, "The flour in the big tin on the cupboard. And the baking powder beside it." She continued drinking her coffee while Phulmattie took some flour out of the tin, using the cup Dularie always left in the tin.

Phulmattie started kneading the dough. She looked at Mohabir and told him, "Mohabir, while you drinking your coffee, cut up the bora."

Mohabir didn't mind being ordered by Dularie. In addition, whenever Dularie wanted him to do something, she would tell him in such a gentle and loving way that he would gladly do it. He resented being ordered by Phulmattie in that manner, but like Dularie, did not know how to respond. Reluctantly, he got up from the table with his coffee, took the small bundle of bora, and started cutting them into small pieces, after washing them.

Phulmattie finished kneading the flour, put the *tawa* on one burner of the fireside, a small *karahi* on the other burner, and poured some oil in the karahi. Then she started flattening the dough.

Dularie looked at her husband and Phulmattie cooking in her kitchen, it evoked all kinds of feelings. *She where I supposed to be. But she and her husband make me drink so much last night, I feel bruck up[44].* The thought of drink made her remember how she felt the previous day, and how she enjoyed breakfast and the ensuing activities, and she thought, *But I don't want to start drinking now. If we start now, they gon want to drink the whole day. Besides, we finish all the rum last night. We don't have any more in the house.*

It appeared as if Mohabir was reading her thoughts, because he said, "Slippery Ochro, a drink gon make us enjoy breakfast. But we finish all the drinks last night."

Phulmattie intervened. "Mohabir, if you give Slippery Ochro some money, he can run quick, quick to Manbahal, and buy a bottle. Slippery Ochro, buy Russian Bear. We lucky with Russian Bear. We gon find a bear inside the cork and get another bottle."

Mohabir hoped that events would play out like it did, because he too remembered how much he enjoyed the previous morning after a few drinks before breakfast. He promptly got up, went into the room, and brought out five dollars which he handed to Slippery Ochro. "You sure you don't want to go to Prashad?" he asked Slippery Ochro.

Slippery Ochro quipped, "Only if Dularie go with me."

Both Mohabir and Dularie stiffened as Slippery Ochro pocketed the five dollars and walked out the door.

Phulmattie baked the roti on the tawa as Dularie remained seated at the table, her head in her hands, trying to cope with the intrusion in their home, in addition to a massive headache. She had drunk a quarter of a cup of coffee, but still felt nauseous, but was afraid of throwing up because of the embarrassment it would cause.

Slippery Ochro must have run to Manbahal's rum shop, because fifteen minutes after he had set out, he opened the door, flourished the bottle like a prize, and placed it in front of Mohabir. Mohabir knew that a bottle of rum cost three dollars, but was too embarrassed to ask Slippery Ochro for the change, and waited in vain for Slippery Ochro to give the change to him.

He not working. Let him keep the change, Mohabir thought.

---

[44] Exhausted

"You open the bottle and look for the bear," Slippery Ochro told him. "You give me the money to buy the bottle, so if you find a bear, you take the free bottle."

Mohabir opened the bottle, then went to the cupboard to get a knife to pry the cardboard cover from under the cork. And Presto! There was a Russian bear staring at him.

"This is a good sign," said Slippery Ochro. "It mean that you and me got good luck together."

"Look how many good things happen since we build our house on your land," Phulmattie added.

Mohabir tried to remember how many good things happened since Slippery Ochro and Phulmattie invaded his property, but could not remember any. Then he thought of Phulmattie on top of him, and smiled as he poured a few drops of rum on the kitchen floor, before pouring for Dularie and himself and passing the bottle to Slippery Ochro.

After the first drink, Slippery Ochro leaned towards Mohabir and told him in a confidential voice, "I glad you tell me last night that you gon support me in my case against Prashad. Not because he own a rum shop and grocery store he can tell anybody anything."

"I can't remember saying that I gon support you in your case with Prashad."

"You had a lot of drinks. Man, I see you pour some heavy drinks last night. You can really hold yuh drinks, you know. You probably can't remember, but I know that you mean it. You told me that, *My word is my bond*. I know that you gon keep your word."

"I can't remember saying that either. I remember telling you when you ask me if I would change my mind about you building your house on my property that my word is my bond."

"You said it again last night, but you had so many drinks that you can't remember." Then Slippery Ochro straightened up, looked at Dularie and Mohabir, and continued, "I know that you always keep your word. Leh we take another drink."

Mohabir and Dularie looked at each other desperately, but neither of them said anything for a while. After they drank their second drink, Mohabir apprehensively asked Slippery Ochro, "So what you want me to do?"

"You say that you gon go and give evidence that Prashad ask you if you take a second wife when he see you with Phulmattie."

"I gon tell the judge that Prashad said that, but I gon say that he was joking."

"Haynes gon argue that, even if he was joking, people in Canal talk about it, and make joke about me. Anyway, you should not buy anything from Prashad shop anymore. Buy from Manbahal."

Dularie, who had perked up after two drinks, intervened. "Since I marry Mohabir, we always buy groceries from Prashad."

Phulmattie decided to make it a woman-to-woman talk. "You don't know, girl. After you give evidence and Prashad got to pay us money, they can put rat poison in your groceries. If they can break the seal of the rum bottle, and water down the rum, they can do anything."

"They won't do that. We been friends for too long." But after she said it, Dularie grimaced as she thought of rat poison eating out the insides of herself and her beloved husband. *They gon really do that?* she thought.

Then she remembered her father's brother, Mohan, who was poisoned by his wife, Dookie. Everybody wondered why he was losing his appetite and was becoming thinner every day, and thought that he was just suffering from anemia, from which he would recover. When he died, they blamed him for not going to the doctor. When they did an autopsy at the Public Hospital, they discovered that he had been slowly poisoned.

The police had gotten a warrant to search the house, but all they could find was a bottle of rat poison, a quarter full. Dookie explained that the house was full of rats, of which she was deathly afraid, and that she was using the rat poison to get rid of them. When the police questioned her why the same type of rat poison was found in her husband's body, she said that she did not know, and that her husband was drinking rum daily, and must have taken the rat poison by mistake.

Although the police was ninety percent sure that Dookie poisoned her husband, they could not get enough evidence to charge her. She remained in the house, which her husband worked hard to pay for. Shortly after, another man from her village moved in with her. All the women in the village knew what she did, but were afraid of her, and warned their husbands not to get too close to her.

A few of them threatened their husbands who got too unruly. "If you don't stop your stupidness, I gon do what Dookie do to her husband." Scared, their husbands would invariably start to behave.

"Why you so quiet?" Slippery Ochro asked Dularie.

Startled, Dularie was tempted to tell them about her uncle, but instinctively knew that this would give Phulmattie and Slippery Ochro more ammunition. "Oh. I been just thinking what Phulmattie said about rat poison. Prashad won't do that."

"Money make people do strange things," Phulmattie said. "Slippery Ochro, tell them how your nephew kill he own father for money."

"He in jail now. He can't spend a red cent of the money," Slippery Ochro responded.

Phulmattie replied, not so much for Slippery Ochro's benefit, but for Dularie's and Mohabir's. "I know. But Dularie and Mohabir too kind. They don't believe a son gon kill his own father for his house and land. But it happen with we own family. If you don't want to go to Manbahal, I gon buy groceries for you." Phulmattie lay her hand on Dularie's arm, and spoke to her soothingly, "I don't want anything to happen to you." Then she got up and went to the fireside to get breakfast for everyone.

Dularie, was touched by this gesture. She smiled and waited for her food to be brought to her. *I worked hard all my life,* she thought. *Now I can sit here, and Phulmattie gon bring my food to me. I can get accustomed to this.* Dularie thought that the roti and bora tasted good, especially after the few drinks, and because of that she did not have to lift a finger to prepare it. After breakfast, they continued drinking, until the bottle was finished.

"You want me to go and get the other bottle now, or we gon wait til this afternoon?" Slippery Ochro asked Mohabir.

"I feel a bit tired. I was going to go to the backdam and do some work, but I got to rest a bit."

"This afternoon then," Slippery Ochro conceded.

Mohabir felt as if he had no choice. "Okay. I gon go and rest now." He looked at Dularie who had perked up quite a bit, and seemed at peace.

"You go and rest," Dularie told her husband. "When Slippery Ochro and Phulmattie leave, I gon put away the dishes and come and rest with you."

"I gon wash the dishes and pack them up. You sit there, Dularie," Phulmattie said. "Or if you want, you can go and rest with Mohabir." She winked at Dularie and smiled lasciviously.

Dularie, well past the stage of euphoria caused by the alcohol, had entered the lethargic stage, especially after the heavy breakfast, and readily accepted Phulmattie's help.

"Close the door when you go out," she said, as she accompanied Mohabir to the bedroom, and promptly fell asleep. She did not hear when Slippery Ochro and Phulmattie closed the back door, and she and Mohabir slept well past noon.

Dularie dreamt that she was getting married to Mohabir for the second time when she was awakened by a knocking. At first, she thought that somebody was knocking on the back door, but when she heard the knocking repeated, it was on the bedroom door. She groaned as she nudged Mohabir with her body and announced, "Phulmattie and Slippery Ochro."

"But they just left."

"It two o'clock," Dularie reminded him.

"You get it," Mohabir told his wife. "I want to sleep some more."

Dularie got up and changed into her house clothes before she opened the bedroom door. She was greeted by a full gold-toothed smile.

"Heh eh, gal! You prappa[45] sleep. Slippery Ochro and me went to the backdam and pull out some eddoes and cassava. And we cut a hand of plantain too. I say that I gon cook for you. What you want? Soup, or Boil and Fry?"

Dularie, too stunned to reply, looked at Mohabir who decided to join them, and noticed that he was scratching his head. and this increased her anxiety. *They come in my house and knock at my bedroom door*, she thought. *Next time, they gon come inside my bedroom.*

"If you can't make up your mind, I gon cook soup," Phulmattie continued. "Slippery Ochro like soup."

This is eye pass, Mohabir thought, and decided to assert himself. "I like boil and fry. I want boil and fry," he told Phulmattie.

Phulmattie awarded him one of her gold-toothed smiles. "You the boss," she told him as she made her way to the kitchen to peel the vegetables. She seemed to be quite comfortable in the kitchen and knew where everything was located. When Dularie joined her, she had already lit the fire and had a pot of water boiling. She had put some salt fish in a

---

[45] Was really "into it"

bowl of water to wash out the salt, and had almost finished peeling all the vegetables. Phulmattie did not look up when she heard Dularie's footsteps, but instructed her, "Dularie, can you cut up some onions and garlic to fry the salt fish? We gon add some turmeric, too. It gon make it taste good."

She helping me out, but who house this? Dularie was again caught in a maelstrom of feelings, as she reached for the onions and garlic, and put them on the cutting board. As she was slicing the onions and garlic, a sudden realization struck her. They don't have food to cook, and they get our own provision and cook for us, so they can eat too. This made her regard Phulmattie taking over of her kitchen in a kinder light. *Let them cook and we gon eat. I don't want them to live on our land and go hungry. If we do that, we gon get sin. We got enough for us and them too. Once they don't take advantage of we.*

Mohabir entered the kitchen at the same time Slippery Ochro came in the back door. Nobody was surprised that he was holding a bottle of Russian Bear in his right hand. "I say that we gon take a few drinks while the provision cooking," he announced to everybody.

"You gon make Mohabir and Dularie into alcoholics," Phulmattie teased, pretending that she didn't know that Slippery Ochro was going to bring the bottle.

"One or two drinks before meals won't matter," Slippery Ochro responded as he put the bottle on the table.

Mohabir scratched his head, briefly, and got up to get glasses and a bottle of Pepsi. Dularie, who was feeling a bit depressed after the effects of the drinks she had taken earlier had worn off, welcomed the drinks, but didn't want to express her desire openly. After Mohabir placed the glasses and Pepsi on the table, Slippery Ochro handed him the sealed bottle of rum. "Here, you take the maiden."

Dularie flushed deeply, while Mohabir took the bottle from Slippery Ochro's hand, and placed it on the table in front of him. He, too, was uncomfortable with the ribaldry in the company of his wife, but was at a loss for words. He opened the bottle and tilted it very carefully so that only a few drops fell on the floor, before pouring for himself and Dularie. Meanwhile, Slippery Ochro was prying the cover under the lid, looking for another imprint of a Russian bear, and scowled when he did not see one. When Mohabir passed the bottle to him, Slippery Ochro, eagerly poured liberal amounts for himself and Phulmattie.

Normally, taking a few drinks while cooking would have been a good experience, but they had already drunk during breakfast, and the complications around Slippery Ochro's impending case with Prashad, threw a cloud over the entire occasion for Mohabir and Dularie. Phulmattie got up frequently from the table to tend to the fire, and put all the ingredients in the pot in a timely manner. Once again, Dularie was pleased that she did not have to do anything, although she had an uncomfortable feeling that she and Mohabir would have to pay for being pampered—something that did not occur to her, until after their third drink.

Slippery Ochro addressed them. "I so glad that we are friends. Nobody can take their eyes pass us. We support each other."

Both Mohabir and Dularie stiffened, and reflected on their lives, which after their marriage could be divided into two stages—before and after Slippery Ochro and Phulmattie came into their lives. Before the couple moved on their property, they did not need any protection from any of the villagers, and they both wondered why they would need protection then.

Slippery Ochro said, "The two of us gon show Prashad that he can't say anything about our wives. Once rumors like that start, the whole of Canal gon think that it is true."

We went through all of that before, Mohabir thought. *And I told him that Prashad was only joking. But he determined to go through with it. And he want to drag me into it. I gon tell the truth and let the judge decide.*

"You all gon eat now?" Phulmattie asked. It was not really a question, because she was already dishing out platefuls of provisions and saltfish, and bringing them to the table.

"Leh we take another drink, and then we gon eat," Slippery Ochro told his wife, but looked at Mohabir and Dularie for confirmation.

Slippery Ochro smiled as Mohabir grabbed the bottle and poured for himself and Dularie, before passing it on to him. With an almost finished bottle of rum and plates of steaming cassava, plantains, eddoes and salt fish in front of them, everybody should have been happy. But Mohabir and Dularie felt a deep sense of discomfort. Although she was enjoying the fact that Phulmattie did all the cooking and serving, Dularie experienced conflicting thoughts. *She taking over my whole house. Next thing I know, she gon want to take me husband. But what can I do?*

Both Dularie and Mohabir had strong survival skills, in that they would persist in spite of difficulties and would disadvantage themselves in order to maintain peace and order. Unfortunately, this trait left them vulnerable to people who liked to exploit others. Dularie could not decide whether she was too nice, or too afraid to put a stop to everything. Whenever she found herself thinking like this, she would start thinking in another trend. This time she thought, *We okay. They don't have much, and they want us to help them. It won't make us poor.* This mantra had an immediate effect, and she started to enjoy her dinner.

Everybody enjoyed the *Boil and Fry*, and Mohabir went so far as to tell Phulmattie, "You know, this boil and fry taste bet..., as good as when Dularie cook it."

Phulmattie flashed her gold teeth exultantly. "I glad you like it. I can cook it whenever you want, but tell me before, so that Slippery Ochro can go and get the provision. You know, we so lucky to live in the country. We can grow our own fruits and vegetables. When people from Georgetown visit their relatives in the country, they ask them, *What you got for me?* And when people from the country go to Georgetown to visit their relatives, their relatives ask them, *What you bring for me?*"

Mohabir smiled cynically as he looked at Slippery Ochro.

Mohabir had enough to drink, and figured that Dularie had more than enough, so was quite prepared to refuse if Slippery Ochro suggested another bottle. However, both Slippery Ochro and Phulmattie promptly left after the meal, leaving Mohabir and Dularie to clear the table, and wash the dishes. They did not mind this, because it gave them some time to talk.

"We drinking too much with Slippery Ochro and Phulmattie," Dularie told her husband as she walked unsteadily to the sink with the plates.

"Yes," Mohabir conceded. "We never used to drink so much before Slippery Ochro and Phulmattie build their house on our land. Today, we just lay down on our bed, nice and quiet, and they come over with a bottle of rum. And once we take one or two, we can't stop."

"Rum don't tell you *Stop*," Dularie observed.

"No! That's why I like to take one or two and then eat. I don't like to drink after I eat."

"But when Slippery Ochro and Phulmattie come, one bottle rum isn't enough for us. Sometimes, you got to go and buy another bottle. We can't continue like this."

"If he win his case with Prashad, he might get enough money to buy his own land. Then if he move out, he won't come here every day with his wife. You got to cook *Boil and Fry* yourself then."

Dularie was incensed. "I cook for you since we married, and you like my cooking. Now that woman cook for you one time, and you been going to say that she cook better than me. You like her cooking better than mine. Why you don't go and *tek she*[46]"

"I just trying to make her feel nice, after she cook for us."

"You ever say something to make me feel nice after I cook for you all these years?"

"So, because I say something nice to her, I must tek she?"

"It look like you like she better than me."

"She never quarrel with me like you do for stupidness."

"Oh, I stupid now. And she smart? I gon sleep in the other bedroom tonight. You can call she over and sleep with she."

Dularie left the kitchen and went in another bedroom, leaving Mohabir to finish clearing the table and washing the dishes. Mohabir had half a mind to go and sleep with his wife in the other bedroom, but did not want her to feel that he was weak.

She gon want to take advantage of me if I show that I can't sleep without she, he thought. *Tomorrow night, she gon want to sleep with me.*

So, for the first time since they got married, except for the times when Dularie was visiting her parents, or when Mohabir was not at home, Mohabir and Dularie slept in separate bedrooms. They lay in their separate beds, tossing and wondering what was happening to their marriage. The alcohol, which they had previously enjoyed in moderate quantities, began to feed their egos, and urged them to find fault with each other.

**

In the morning, they went into the kitchen. Mohabir was happy that he had taken the time the previous night to clear the table and wash the dishes. He decided to take the initiative and start breakfast, and he put the water on the fireside to boil for coffee on one burner and the karahi on the other. After he put some oil in the karahi, he looked at Dularie for the first time since they entered the kitchen. "You want boulangers or seme[47]?"

Dularie was relieved that she did not have to speak first. "Some salt fish left over from last night. Let we finish that. I gon cook some roti," she said as she went to the container to take out enough flour to make two rotis.

---

[46] Live home with her
[47] A type of green bean

Mohabir smiled, as he realized that things were going to be all right between him and his wife. "While the water is boiling, you want me to go and pick some tangerines from the tree that bear sweet tangerines?"

"Leh we drink coffee now, and we can have the tangerine about ten o'clock."

Chapter 7

"Home is where we should feel secure and comfortable."
—Catherine Pulsifer—

Mohabir and Dularie prepared breakfast, and neither talked about the incidents that occurred the previous night. Although both experienced mild hangovers, both knew that their behavior the previous night was atypical, and both silently acknowledged that alcohol was a major factor. Dularie kneaded the flour and made the rotis, while Mohabir made the coffee and warmed up the salt-fish.

When everything was on the table, and they were about to take the first mouthful, the knocking on the back door made Dularie groan. Mohabir scratched his head furiously, and they said simultaneously, "Slippery Ochro or Phulmattie."

Mohabir welcomed the interruption, because it meant that he did not have to deal with the misunderstanding he had with Dularie the previous night. It was different for Dularie, who thought, *The woman take over my kitchen last night, and she come to take it over again. I have to put a stop to this.*

When she opened the door, there was Phulmattie holding four tangerines.

"I know you like tangerines, especially after you take a few drinks," she told Dularie. "I ask Slippery Ochro to pick some from your favorite tree. What you cooking for breakfast?"

Mohabir had joined them at the door and answered for her. "We eating roti and the salt-fish left over from last night."

"Slippery Ochro and me eat callaloo and roti. Some callaloo left over. After all, is you own callaloo. I pick some from you garden this morning. I know that you won't mind." She flashed her gold teeth at Mohabir. "You want me to help you in the garden this morning? Or we can do some work in the backdam."

Mohabir, who had stopped scratching his head for a while, resumed the scratching as he looked at Dularie for rescue.

Dularie reached out for the tangerines, gave them to Mohabir, and told Phulmattie, "Thanks for the tangerine. I hope that you pick some for yourself and Slippery Ochro." She did not pause for a reply, because she already knew the answer. "The salt fish and roti enough for us. Mohabir and me gon work in the garden this afternoon. We just start eating, and the roti getting cold."

Both were relieved when Phulmattie took the hint. "I gon leave you two love birds to finish your breakfast," she told them as she left.

It was this parting sentence that motivated Mohabir and Dularie to forget about their differences the previous night. They had been called "love birds" by many people before, and being called this again reminded them of how close they were. "Like she read your mind," Mohabir said. "She bring your favorite tangerine for you."

"They ask us to build their house on our land. Now they picking our fruits and reaping we vegetables."

"She did offer to help in the garden," Mohabir replied placatingly.

"They gon help us plant on our land, and help us reap on our land. They gon be partners with us, just because we allow them to build their house on our land."

Mohabir started to scratch his head, because he knew that Dularie was speaking the truth, and Dularie, fearing for his well-being, conceded, "But we got all this land, and we getting old. It good that they helping out."

"You right. But when people want take their finger and juk out you eye, you got to put a stop to it." But even as he said it, both Mohabir and Dularie knew that they did not have the courage to do anything about the situation, and that they would allow Slippery Ochro and Phulmattie to continue living on their land and intrude in their lives, convincing themselves that they were doing something good by helping a couple in need.

**

About two months later, while Mohabir and Dularie were having a nap after lunch, there was a knock at the back door. They did not usually lock their doors during the day, even while they were napping, but they did not appreciate Slippery Ochro and Phulmattie walking into their house and knocking on their bedroom door, so they resorted to locking both doors, when they wanted to rest after lunch. Groggily, Mohabir went to the back door, opened it, and saw Slippery Ochro gleefully holding a letter in his hand like someone holding a winning lottery ticket.

"Haynes write me. The court case next month." The joy on Slippery Ochro's face was indescribable, and in sharp contrast to the consternation on Mohabir's.

He and Dularie had made an effort to forget about the case in the hope that it would go away, that the lawyer would say that it was not worth pursuing, or the slim chance that Slippery Ochro would change his mind. Mohabir could not imagine that he would have to give evidence against his friend, Prashad.

Slippery Ochro reminded him of this painful fact. "Haynes said that he gon issue a summons for you to appear in court, so you can always tell Prashad that the court summons you, and you got to go to court and give evidence."

Mohabir scratched his head vigorously, and turned to Dularie, who was staring at Slippery Ochro as if lost in a trance. The uncomfortable silence lasted for a long while.

Dularie summoned enough courage to tell Slippery Ochro, "Mohabir and Prashad been friends since before we get married. Now you want him to give evidence against Prashad in court."

"All he got to do is tell the truth that Prashad tell him that it look as if he take me wife as his second wife."

Mohabir repeated what he had said a number of times. "Prashad was only joking."

"Let him joke about he own wife, not me wife," Slippery Ochro countered.

Dularie looked at the kiskadees, blue sakis and hummingbirds frolicking among the branches of the star-apple tree not far from the house. "They so happy," she said.

Mohabir, who felt anything but happy, and Slippery Ochro, who was on cloud nine and still brandishing the letter, both asked, "Who happy?"

Dularie pointed to the star-apple tree, covered in flowers. "The birds. They don't have a care in the world."

"Prashad gon have plenty trouble next month when the court case come up," Slippery Ochro said.

There was an uncomfortable silence for a few moments, as Mohabir and Dularie looked at each other.

Slippery Ochro leaned over to Mohabir and whispered conspiratorially, "I gon go to Manbahal and take a few drinks to celebrate. You want to come with me? Or I can buy a bottle and bring it here, so that Phulmattie and Dularie can have some drinks too."

Mohabir did not want to go with Slippery Ochro anywhere, but thought of all the evenings when Dularie drank more that she should have. He did not want Slippery Ochro to bring a bottle of rum to his house, and rationalized that he was protecting Dularie by going with Slippery Ochro to drink at Manbahal. "All right! We gon go to Manbahal and take a quick drink. But I don't know what we got to celebrate. Prashad is me friend."

"So, your friend encourage you to take me wife as your second wife?"

"The man been just joking."

"Many a true thing pass as joke," Slippery Ochro repeated.

Mohabir thought of replying, but then he remembered his tryst with Phulmattie and decided not to say anything.

"I gon pick you up at about five," Slippery Ochro told him as he left.

As soon as Slippery was out of earshot, Mohabir turned to Dularie. "I know that you don't like to drink with Slippery Ochro and Phulmattie, because they don't know when to stop. That why I gon go with Slippery Ochro to drink at Manbahal."

"You right! I don't like drinking with them. But you don't got to use that as an excuse to go drinking with Slippery Ochro, either. That man like a razor blade. He cut both sides. You better be careful, before he turn on you."

"I live a straight life. How he gon turn on me?"

"He already causing problems between you and Prashad."

"I still talking to Prashad. Before I go to Manbahal, I gon go to Prashad and tell him I gon tell the court that he was just joking."

"You always saying that, but it depend on what the judge think." But she relented when she saw Mohabir starting to scratch his head as he tried to think of an appropriate answer. "Just tell the truth. Slippery Ochro and Phulmattie just trying to make trouble. When you go drink with Slippery Ochro at Manbahal, don't talk anything about Prashad, or else everybody in Canal gon know. Slippery Ochro tell you when the court date is?"

Mohabir realized that he had forgotten to ask when the court date was, but remembered that Slippery Ochro told him that he would get a court summons to appear as a witness. "Slippery Ochro say that I gon get a summons to appear. The summons gon have the date."

"Police never come to our house since we get married, and now police gon come because we allow Slippery Ochro and Phulmattie to build they house on we land."

"They just summoning me as a witness. They not charging me with anything. I gon ask Slippery Ochro when is the court date when I see him this afternoon. Leh we go and rest a bit now."

Dularie was surprised at her husband's suggestion. "You expect me to go and rest after this!"

Mohabir was also too excited to relax, but did not know what to do before going to Manbahal. "You're right," he replied. "I gon go to Prashad and explain what happening. He gon understand."

"I got to buy some groceries, so I gon go with you. I don't want us to make bad with Prashad. We know him for a long time. He is a nice and good man."

"Yes!" Mohabir agreed. "He is my friend, and now I got to give evidence against him."

**

The sun shone brightly as Mohabir and Dularie walked to Prashad's shop, and as they looked at people puttering about in their yards, or relaxing in their hammocks under their houses, they wondered how everybody could relax when there was so much trouble in the air. When they reached Prashad, there was nobody in the grocery section, but two tables were occupied in the rum shop section.

Mohan, one of the drinkers, called out to Mohabir. "Hey, Mohabir, I didn't see you for a long time, man. Come tek a lil drink wid[48] me."

Mohan was wearing trousers torn at both knees, and the front of his shirt was knotted in front. The top two buttons of his shirt were undone. Mohabir smiled when he saw this, and remembered that Mohan liked to show off the thick black hair on his chest.

Mohabir did not feel like drinking. Besides, he really wanted to talk with Prashad about the court case, but felt that Mohan would think that he was playing a big shot if he did not go. He turned to Dularie, "You buy your

---

[48] with

groceries. I gon take a quick drink and then come back and we can talk to Prashad about the case."

Dularie knew it was useless to argue, and waited in the grocery section because Prashad was busy in the rum shop. Prashad did not greet Mohabir when he entered the rum shop section, and Mohabir immediately knew that Prashad was aware of, and angry about the court case. As Mohabir walked towards him, Prashad, without initiating eye contact, retreated to the grocery section. Frustrated, Mohabir took the glass which Mohan had asked for, and poured a drink. "I can take one drink with you all. Then I got to go and talk to Prashad."

"Prashad frighten to talk with you," Mohan explained. "He say that *he spirit gon from you*[49], and he frighten to tell you, 'Good Morning!' He said that he don't want to get sued again."

Mohabir scratched his head as he told Mohan, "Oh my God! He think that I start it? I didn't do or say anything. Slippery Ochro go to see his lawyer, and they start it. I just going to be a witness."

"But what you say on the witness stand can cost him his house and land."

"I gon go and talk with him now, and explain." Mohabir drained his glass and made his way to the grocery section. Prashad was talking to Dularie when he entered, and he just caught the end of the sentence "... just joking with him." Prashad made an attempt to go to the rum shop section when Mohabir walked in, but Mohabir pre-empted him. "Prashad, I want to talk with you."

When Prashad turned around reluctantly, Mohabir saw that he was dressed very formally, with a grey pair of trousers, so very carefully ironed that the creases were prominent. Instead of a sports shirt, he wore a starched white shirt-jac. His features were very stern and formal, almost as if he was preparing for the court trial.

"You want to talk with me? Why don't you go and talk with your tenant and friend, Slippery Ochro?"

"Me and you been friends longer than me and Slippery Ochro."

"That's why you giving evidence against me?"

"I gon tell the judge what you say, but I gon explain that you been just joking."

---

[49] He doesn't like you any more

"They gon ask you how you know that I been just joking."

"Me and you always joke and tease each other."

Prashad's features softened a bit at this, and there was even a hint of a smile on his lips as he remembered the jokes and teasing that passed between him and Mohabir. "Is your fault for letting Slippery Ochro build his house on your land. You know Slippery Ochro like goat shit. Goat shit only wait for a lil breeze to blow, then it start to roll."

"I let them build their house on my land because I feel sorry for them. They tell me that they just want to build a shelter so that sun don't burn them, and rain don't wet them."

"You feel sorry for his wife." Prashad realized his mistake and quickly corrected himself. "You feel sorry for him and his wife? And you don't feel sorry that he taking me to court? Now, Slippery Ochro want to take me to court to get money from me. That lil joke I make with you gon cost me a lot of money. I got to close the store to go to court, and I got to hire a lawyer."

"I sorry, but I didn't tell Slippery Ochro anything. As soon as we go back home after we buy the rum, Phulmattie tell him. I tell him that you been just joking, but the man determine to go to court."

Mohabir decided that it was an appropriate time to stroke Prashad's ego. "But Slippery Ochro is no match for you. He, too, got to pay a lawyer. And you can hire a good lawyer who can show that you been just joking."

Prashad stood a bit straighter. "I gon hire Looku pon he rass. If he think he bad. Looku gon show him. And his wife too. Why she come with you to buy rum, and cause trouble? You ask she to come with you?"

The lifting of Prashad's spirits was also beneficial to Mohabir, who ignored Prashad's question. "I gon say what you tell me, but when Looku cross examine me, I gon say that we always tease each other, and that you been just joking."

"All right," said Prashad. "Leh we go and take a drink with Mohan and dem boys. I know that you won't turn against me. We gon let Looku and the lawyer that Slippery Ochro hire fight it out. Looku don't lose many case in Guyana."

"Haynes," Mohabir added. "He hire Haynes."

Prashad frowned, and became serious "He hire Haynes? Haynes work on commission, and he ask for big money."

"Yes, but he can't win this case, if I say that you been only joking. Leh we go and take a drink. Bring a half for me."

Mohabir looked at Dularie, who had already bought the groceries that she needed. "You go home with the groceries. I gon come later." Then he realized that Dularie could not carry all the groceries home. "Carry what you can, and I gon bring the rest home, after I take one or two with the boys."

"I happy that you and Prashad still friends, but don't drink too much." She picked up some groceries to take home. "I gon leave the rice and the oil for you. You still gon go out and drink with Slippery Ochro this afternoon?"

"I forget all about Slippery Ochro. In any case, I gon have just one or two, and then come home. I gon talk with Prashad and try to make peace between him and Slippery Ochro."

Dularie looked at the kind, helpful, peace-loving man, whom she called her husband, with tears in her eyes. "I hope that you can make peace. I know that Prashad gon be willing, but people tell me about Slippery Ochro. He like court and he like trouble, and he drag you into it."

"I gon talk with Prashad now, and I gon talk with Slippery Ochro later, and try to make peace. I think that everything gon be all right."

Dularie smiled and left to make her way home, praying that her husband won't be dragged into court.

Mohabir made his way to the rum shop section to join Mohan and the others. Prashad already had a drink in his glass by the time he arrived, so Mohabir took his shot glass from his shirt pocket.

"What happen? You think that we gon poison you?" Satesh, a lean and dark man, a face full of hair, and wearing a straw hat, asked him.

Mohan came to Mohabir's rescue. "Mohabir always keep his glass in his pocket, ever since somebody put poison in Bahadur glass and he nearly dead. They never find out who did it, but Bahadur don't drink in the rum shop anymore. We all should keep our glass in we pocket, so if somebody get sick, he can't say that we poison them."

That put an end to any criticism, and everybody was quiet until Mohabir poured and raised his glass. "To all my friends," he toasted as they raised their glasses. They drained their glasses. Mohabir turned to Prashad, "I gon talk to Slippery Ochro this afternoon, and I gon try to get him to come to your place. You can explain that you been only joking, and that he should drop the court case."

"Slippery Ochro get his sweetness from court case, but if you can get him to come, I gon put a bottle of whisky on the table, and we can talk."

"I gon try my best. Let me take one last drink, and then go. If you see me later, don't be surprised."

Mohabir was happy that Prashad understood his situation, and was ready to talk with Slippery Ochro, but knew instinctively that Slippery Ochro would not talk to Prashad. *He gon only talk to Prashad if Prashad agree to give him his house and land*, he said to himself, as he slowly walked home with the rice and oil.

He found Dularie in the kitchen. She had prepared a dinner of curried eggs and potatoes and roti, and was waiting on Mohabir to eat.

She told her husband, "So Prashad understand that you did not turn against him. Slippery Ochro come earlier and I tell he that you gon come home in a while. You gon eat now?"

"Let me go and take a few drinks with Slippery Ochro. I tell Prashad that I gon talk with Slippery Ochro, and try to take him to Prashad so that they can talk to each other and come to a settlement."

"You want Prashad to give Slippery Ochro his house and land? That the only way Slippery Ochro gon settle."

"Oh my God! We living together for too long. I been telling myself the same thing when I been walking home. But I still got to try."

"You better eat something before you go, or else you can get drunk."

A knock on the door interrupted them, and when Mohabir opened the door, Slippery Ochro and Phulmattie were standing on the top step. Slippery Ochro was dressed in a flowered shirt which he wore over his beige trousers, and his old Wilson hat with an artificial flower in the head band, while Phulmattie was dressed in a plain grey dress and a blue embroidered rumal. Both Dularie and Mohabir were surprised to see a half-full twenty-six-ounce bottle of rum in her right hand.

Phulmattie said, in what Dularie considered a brazen tone, "I say that me and you gon take a lil drink while Mohabir and Slippery Ochro go to Manbahal. We got mouth to drink, too."

Dularie was confounded and speechless, while Slippery Ochro turned to Mohabir. "You ready? Snakeskin and Dugdug gon meet us at Manbahal. They must be there already, because we late."

"Leh we go. I just talked with Prashad, and I want to talk with you, too," Mohabir said.

"You talk with Prashad? I thought that you and me on the same side."

"I want to make peace between you and Prashad. We live in Canal. We can settle any problems between us. We don't need to go to no court."

Slippery Ochro looked at Mohabir with an unbelieving gaze. "You want me to settle with Prashad? You gon pay Haynes? Mohabir, I invite you for a drink, man. Leh we go take a drink. But don't talk stupidness."

Chapter 8

"There was a sound in their voices which suggested rum."

—Robert Louis Stevenson—

Mohabir knew it was hopeless to come to any agreement with Slippery Ochro, and remained quiet as he walked down the stairs to go to Manbahal. The sun was setting as they wended their way on the dirt road leading to the bridge across the canal. They could not see a soul in sight—most people were at home preparing dinner, eating dinner, or relaxing after dinner.

They crossed Gobin's bridge in silence, until they reached Manbahal's rum shop, when Slippery Ochro observed, "Snakeskin and Dugdug here already."

Mohabir saw the two men with a quarter bottle of rum at a table, and knew that they bought the small bottle just to kill time until he and Slippery Ochro arrived.

Slippery Ochro went to the counter and ordered a bottle of Russian Bear rum, four bottles of Pepsi, and two glasses. He fetched the rum, while Mohabir took the glasses and they joined the two men at the table.

Slippery Ochro pulled out the letter from his shirt pocket. "I got Prashad where I want him now," he remarked to Snakeskin and Dugdug. "He gon learn that he can't go around making remarks about people wife."

Dugdug looked at the letter, and turned to Snakeskin, "The court case next month."

"Yes. Read the letter. Haynes say that they gon hear the case on the twenty-fourth of next month. Mohabir gon give witness that Prashad tell he that he take my wife as his second wife."

Mohabir had heard Slippery Ochro's accusation so often that his response was automatic. "Prashad was only joking."

"Well, he can make joke when he sign over his house and land to Slippery Ochro. You don't make a joke like that about a man wife," Snakeskin told Mohabir.

"We poor, but we don't let people take their ass pass us," Slippery Ochro told the group. "Phulmattie tell me that since we got married, another man never hold she hand, and I believe her. We think the same way. We try to help people whenever we can."

He opened the bottle and checked the inside of the cork, and not finding an image of a bear, threw a little bit of rum on the floor for absent friends, and poured for himself and Mohabir, before pushing the bottle towards Snakeskin and Dugdug. They had some rum left from the quarter bottle they had bought, and while Slippery Ochro was pouring, they were in the process of draining their glasses in anticipation of drinking from the new bottle.

"It gon serve Prashad right," Dugdug remarked as he poured a drink from the fresh bottle. "He refuse to give me wife credit when she go to buy some flour and rice. And we only owe him a little bit. We tell him that me wife father sick, and he gon die soon. She is his only child, and we gon pay him as soon as he die, and we inherit some money. Prashad say that he can't wait for somebody to die before he get his money. Take his ass to court, Slippery Ochro."

"He refuse to give me rum on credit, too," Snakeskin said. "Me and them boys been drinking, and we want another bottle, but nobody had any money. I ask the man for a bottle on credit, but he refuse. He say that I already owe him money for rum. Yes, I owe him, but I gon pay him when I get money."

Mohabir was tempted to ask him where he will get the money from, because he knew that Snakeskin, like Dugdug and Slippery Ochro, was not working. Snakeskin's wife, a slim, but tough woman, who liked to always be in control, earned some money by keeping two cows, and selling their milk. In addition, she kept a flourishing vegetable garden, amply nourished by cow dung, which produced enough vegetables for their own consumption, with enough left over to sell to neighbors. This gave her enough money to buy flour, salt, sugar and other essentials from the grocery store.

On rare occasions, Snakeskin would cut a bundle of grass for the cows, but on most days, he would lie in the hammock and say that he felt as if he was going to die any time. At first, when he started complaining, he garnered a great deal of sympathy, but like the boy who cried *Wolf*, his wife learned to ignore his complaints. Snakeskin sometimes got a few dollars from his *sweet woman*, a buxom woman who owned a cake shop and who lived a few doors from his home. Her husband had died, leaving her with one daughter, who tended to the cake shop whenever her mother went to keep her rendezvous with Snakeskin.

Mohabir was not surprised that Slippery Ochro, Snakeskin and Dugdug were friends, and wondered how he ended up in such company. He decided to make a last attempt to bring peace between Slippery Ochro and Prashad. As he reached for the bottle, poured a drink for himself, and passed the bottle to Slippery Ochro, he told him, "Prashad say that he gon put a bottle of whisky on the table, and apologize to you if we go to his place."

Slippery Ochro was about to pour a drink but he put the bottle down, and looked at Mohabir intensely. "You think that I scraven[50] for whisky?" he asked Mohabir in an angry tone. "You know how many bottle whisky I can buy when I get my settlement from Prashad?"

"I just trying to make peace," Mohabir said weakly.

Slippery Ochro replied in a tone of finality, "I gon make peace after I get my settlement in court," as he poured a large drink for himself before passing the bottle to Snakeskin.

While they were drinking, Baba and his wife came to buy some groceries and they saw Mohabir drinking with Slippery Ochro, Snakeskin and Dugdug. His wife, a very religious lady named Sita, who always wore an orhni, instead of a rumal, and who had requested the involvement of the Panchayat in the village, turned to her husband. "What Mohabir doing drinking with those *lungeras*[51]?"

"He allow Slippery Ochro to build his house on his land," Baba, a tall thin man, who earned the reputation in the village of being a hard-working man, replied. "Everybody in Canal respect Mohabir, but if he start to follow Slippery Ochro and his friends, he gon lose respect in the village. Mohabir always take a drink or two at Prashad with Mohan and them boys, but now he drinking at Manbahal with Slippery Ochro and his friends." Then he remembered the rumor he had heard. "I hear that Slippery Ochro taking Prashad to court and that Mohabir going to give witness against Prashad."

---

[50] hungish
[51] Bums

"But Mohabir and Prashad been friends for a long time. I didn't think that anything can come between them."

"You don't know Slippery Ochro and Phulmattie. They can make trouble between Ram and Sita."

"You making fun of Ram and Sita?"

"No! I just saying that you don't know Slippery Ochro and Phulmattie. They live for trouble and court. They happiest when they at court. Mohabir gon regret letting Slippery Ochro and Phulmattie build their house on their land."

"It don't look like he regretting it now. It look like he having a good time."

"Wha a sweeten goat mouth gon hurt he belly," Baba said. "Let me go and talk with Mohabir a bit."

"You want to go and drink with Mohabir, Slippery Ochro, Snakeskin and Dugdug? We just talk about how Mohabir keeping bad company. Now you want to join them?"

"I gon just say, *Hello*. Not because Mohabir drink with Slippery Ochro and his friends, I gon stop talking to him. Everybody in Canal respect him."

"All right, you go and talk with him. You can tell him that if he follow Slippery Ochro and his lungera friends, people will lose respect for him. And for Dularie too."

Baba went into the rum shop section and approached Mohabir. As soon as he saw Baba approaching, Slippery Ochro got up and went to the counter to get another glass.

Baba said, "Mohabir, you always drink at Prashad. How come you drinking here?"

"You want to tell the man where to drink?" This came from Dugdug, who considered Mohabir a friend, and he wasn't going to allow anybody to criticize his friend's choice of rum shops.

Baba was immediately on the defensive. "I didn't mean anything by it.. I just trying to make talk."

By then, Slippery Ochro returned to the table with an extra glass. "Take a drink wid we," he said, as he handed Baba the glass. Baba accepted the glass, intending to take only one drink. He poured a tall drink and drank with the company. As he got up to leave, Dugdug put his hand on his arm.

"What happen? Suddenly you become a one-foot man. You leaving after one drink. You gon hop out of here on one foot?"

Feeling chastised, Baba sat down, and Slippery Ochro passed him the bottle. After he drained the bottle, Baba had an irrational feeling that it was incumbent on him to replace it.

Sita was surprised when she saw her husband at the counter asking Manbahal for another bottle, but did not want to embarrass him by saying anything, and contented herself by chatting with Manbahal's wife, Sumintra, a slim, fair-skinned woman, who many people observed was older than Manbahal, but looked younger because she was so thin, and because she went to a hairdresser in Georgetown once a month to perm and dye her hair. The men in the rum shop section would have liked to be served by her, but Manbahal absolutely prohibited her from serving in the rum shop section.

"You want to go in the rum shop section and let all the drunken people undress you with their eyes?" he had asked her when she offered to help.

Sita turned to Sumintra when she saw her husband walking back with the bottle, and said, "I don't mind when Baba take one or two drink. If he drink with Mohabir alone, that okay, but if he drink with Slippery Ochro and his friends, he gon end up in trouble."

"Slippery Ochro and his friends only talk about how they can get money from people," Sumintra whispered. "Baba just buy another bottle. You better go home now. I gon tell Baba, and he can come when they finish the bottle."

"Baba and me come nice-nice to buy grocery. He always go home with me when we buy grocery. I don't know what bad habit he starting."

Sumintra said, "We can sit and talk if you like, and wait till Baba finish drinking. You want a soft drink? Or I can make a cup of tea."

"I gon go home now. Baba gon get it good tomorrow morning. Me and he come in here nice and peaceful together, and now me alone going home." Sita picked up her groceries and walked out of the store, ignoring Baba, who was waving to her. Out of the corner of her eyes, she could see her husband holding up both hands with ten fingers outstretched. *Ten minutes will turn to an hour*, Sita thought, as she walked out of the store without making full eye contact with her husband.

Baba was upset that his wife left without him, and when Slippery Ochro noticed that he was quiet for a while, he questioned him. "Why you so quiet? It because your wife left? Come take a drink, man. She wearing the pants in yuh home, or you wearing the pants? Women got to learn their place."

"Sita and I always work together," Baba countered. "We pull together, not against each other. That's why we get up a little."

"Phulmattie and me pull together too, but when it come to taking a few drinks with my friends, she don't object."

It was on the tip of Baba's tongue to tell Slippery Ochro that he and Phulmattie are pulling together to take things from other people and to take people to court, but he didn't. Like almost everybody in the village, he was afraid of Slippery Ochro. He said, "Sita like when I take a drink or two at home before dinner. She take one or two with me. But we come together to buy groceries, and now I leave her to take the groceries home alone."

Without thinking, Mohabir joined in the conversation. "It the same with Dularie and me. We use to take only one or two drinks before dinner, until...". He looked at Slippery Ochro, and did not know how to continue.

"You mean I make you and Dularie drink?" Slippery Ochro asked Mohabir.

Mohabir sensed an impending conflict. In the past, he always avoided any conflict, even if it meant that people would take advantage of him. "You know when you got company, you drink more," he replied.

Slippery Ochro conceded. "That true. We got good company now. But when you got company like Prashad, who make fun of yuh wife, that different."

Dugdug decided to declare his support for Slippery Ochro. "That's why you gon sue his ass. I gon come to court to support you. You gon come, Snakeskin?"

"Sure, I gon come. We gon show Prashad that we don't care about his money. We gon show him that friends more important than money." Then he turned to Mohabir. "What about you, Mohabir? You gon come to support Slippery Ochro?"

"When I get summons, I got to go," Mohabir responded, and felt like a broken record when he repeated, "But I gon say that Prashad been only joking when he say that it look like I take Phulmattie for a second wife. Prashad and I always joking."

Dugdug was so incensed that he put his glass on the table and leaned as far back as he could so that he could distance himself from Mohabir, who sat opposite him. "You mean that you gon support Prashad so that he won't have to give Slippery Ochro any money. You think that because you got some money, you can take advantage of poor people like me and Slippery Ochro."

Baba made the mistake of saying, "Dugdug, Mohabir only say that he gon tell the truth that Prashad been only joking."

"You siding with Prashad and Mohabir?" This came from Snakeskin, who regarded it as a war between the rich and poor. "You give it to him good, Dugdug. Not because we poor they can take advantage of we."

Thus supported, Dugdug's anger was inflamed. Eyes red, he grabbed the large bottle which contained water for chasers, being careful not to tip the one which had the rum, and raised it above his head, as he turned to face Baba. "Don't make me behave IGNORANT, and knock you on yuh head with this bottle."

Slippery Ochro looked on with a self-satisfied smile. *I won't say anything. Let Snakeskin and Dugdug handle Mohabir and Baba*, he said to himself.

Baba turned to Mohabir, who was red in the face and was furiously scratching his head. "I just come to take a drink or two with you, and look what happen," he said in a somewhat accusing tone. Feeling very nervous, he added, "Sita did not want me to come, because of the company you keep."

Mohabir turned to Slippery Ochro and said, "I come to take a drink with you, but I also tell you that I gon speak the truth about what Prashad tell me about Phulmattie. Baba join we because me and he are friends. Now Snakeskin and Dugdug want to pick a fight with us. I ain't no fight man. Baba ain't no fight man. All we want to do is take a quiet drink."

Slippery Ochro looked at Mohabir with a sly smile, but ignored his plea for help. Instead, he turned to Snakeskin and Dugdug and winked.

Dugdug, full of Dutch courage, and encouraged by Slippery Ochro, got up from his seat and went across the table to Baba, grabbing him by the front of his shirt. Dugdug brought his face so close to Baba, that Baba could see his missing front teeth and his rotten molars. His breath reeked of alcohol, and Baba sensed that Dugdug did not brush his teeth that morning.

"Leh we see if yuh money can help you now," Dugdug screamed. Baba was trembling with fear and shame. He had witnessed many fights in different rum shops, but never imagined that he would be in one, and looked to Slippery Ochro for help. But Slippery Ochro just sat and looked on with a smile.

Mohabir came and stood by Baba's side, but was afraid to touch Dugdug. "Dugdug, Baba didn't do you anything, man. Why you picking a fight with him?"

Dugdug released his hold on Baba and decided to vent his rage on Mohabir, who was also an initiate to rum shop fights. Holding Mohabir by the front of his shirt, and jerking him closer, Dugdug shouted, "Prashad say that you want to take Slippery Ochro wife as yuh second wife. You want to take my wife as yuh third wife?"

Mohabir did not know how to respond, and decided to keep quiet.

He and Baba were saved by Papas, a strapping twenty-year-old, whose rippling muscles were the envy of most of the men in Canal. Mohabir and the Panchayat had intervened, and ruled favorably for Papas' family when their neighbor wanted to pick the oranges from the tree near the boundary of the land owned by the Papas family.

Papas pinned both of Dugdug's arms, lifted him and moved him away from Mohabir. "You want to fight?" he asked Dugdug. "You can fight me if you want. Don't pick on a man who everybody respect and don't like to fight. Call me any time you want to fight. Don't let me hear that you pick fight with Mohabir anymore." He released Dugdug, who submissively went to sit near Snakeskin. Both knew better than to pick a fight with Papas.

"Leh we go home," Baba told Mohabir. "When Sita hear of this, I gon get it good. And you got to deal with Dularie when you go home. What you gon tell her?"

Because Slippery Ochro was there, Mohabir could not say exactly what was on his mind, so he gave a non-committal reply. "Dularie know that I coming to have a drink with Slippery Ochro. So long now, I been coming to Prashad and Manbahal to take a drink with my friends, I never land in a fight. And look what happen now. Dularie gon be shocked."

He thought, *Dularie told me that if I continue drinking with Slippery Ochro, something like this gon happen. I still continue to drink with Slippery Ochro. I need somebody to wring me ears.*

Emboldened by Papas' presence, Baba said. "Sita didn't want me to come and drink. Not because of you," he told Mohabir. "Now when I go home, I got to tell her what happened. She gon hear about it anyhow. You know how news spread in Canal. If Papas wouldn'a have come in who knows what would'a happen. I might have to take karate classes now," he concluded, as he looked at Dugdug and Snakeskin, who were very subdued.

Slippery Ochro watched in interest, as a director/producer would watch as a play developed, and was pleased with the result. But then he remembered that he was living on Mohabir's land. Turning to Mohabir, he said, "Leh we go home now. I don't know why Dugdug and Snakeskin drink so much and behave like jackasses. Next time when we come out for a drink, I won't invite them."

Mohabir looked at Dugdug and Snakeskin glaring at him, and decided that he would be safer in the company of Slippery Ochro. "All right!" he said. "Let we go right now."

"Uncle Mohabir," Papas told Mohabir, "Don't worry. Dugdug and Snakeskin can't leave this rum shop and follow you. If they want to fight, they can fight me. You sit down right there," he told the two. "When Uncle Mohabir reach home, then you can go home. Or you can fight each other if you still want to fight."

Mohabir left with Slippery Ochro, while Papas stayed behind to ensure that Dugdug and Snakeskin remained.

As soon as they were out of earshot, Slippery Ochro told Mohabir, "If Papas wouldn't a come in, I would'a handle Dugdug and Snakeskin."

Mohabir thought: *You can say anything now. But I didn't hear you saying anything to stop them when they want to fight me and Baba.* He wisely decided not to answer Slippery Ochro, and they both remained silent until they reached Slippery Ochro's home.

Before Slippery Ochro turned to cross the plank across the four-foot drain to go to his home, he asked Mohabir, "You want me to follow you home?"

"I don't think that Dugdug and Snakeskin gon be between here and my house. I gon be okay, but I don't know what to tell Dularie."

"Don't tell her anything tonight. I gon come tomorrow morning and we will tell her together."

The last thing Mohabir wanted was to have Slippery Ochro come over to his house first thing in the morning. "I will not tell her anything tonight, or else she will not sleep. I gon she her after we eat breakfast, but I want to tell her by myself. I don't want anyone with me."

"I gon ask Phulmattie to come over. You know, women understand these things."

The man will not take 'no' for an answer. Next thing he gon want is to send Phulmattie to my bed. "I want to tell Dularie by myself," Mohabir repeated.

"Okay, but I gon still come by later, and find out how things go. I know she gon be angry, but I gon tell her that it not your fault. It was Dugdug and Snakeskin who pick the fight with you."

Mohabir was in a dilemma. He didn't want Slippery Ochro to come to his house, but he was not rude by nature, and did not know what to say to discourage him from visiting. However, he realized that Slippery Ochro was over-stepping his bounds and he remembered that the man did not really do anything to stop Dugdug and Snakeskin when they were picking a fight with him and Baba.

"When Dularie hear what happen, I don't think that she gon want anybody to visit," he told Slippery Ochro to assert himself, and walked towards his house, leaving Slippery Ochro no alternative but to go to his own house. When he walked through the door, he saw Dularie lying on the sofa, and knew that she had a few drinks with Phulmattie, and wanted to rest.

She took one look at his face and told him, "You look upset. What happen with you and Slippery Ochro?"

"Nothing happen between me and Slippery Ochro," Mohabir answered evasively. "Me and Slippery Ochro just came home."

"We been married for so long, and you still think that you can fool me. I know you *too good*. Something bothering you. What happen?"

Mohabir knew that it was useless to argue, because he was aware that Dularie knew him better than he knew himself. "It just that Dugdug and Snakeskin making fools of themselves."

"What they do? Everybody respect you in Canal, never mind how they rich or poor. Nobody got any reason to quarrel with you. What happen with them?"

"They feel that I siding with Prashad when I tell them that I gon say in court that Prashad been only joking when he say that it look like I take a second wife when he see me with Phulmattie."

Dularie's face showed that she was still puzzled. "But you always say that you gon give evidence that Prashad been only joking. You even tell Slippery Ochro that."

Mohabir did not know what to tell his wife, and began to scratch his head furiously until Dularie got up and restrained him. Still holding his hands, she pulled him close to her, and looking intensely in his eyes, led him to the kitchen table. Then she gently exerted pressure on his shoulders and told him to sit. Still holding her husband's hands, she sat in the chair next to him, leaned forward so that her face was almost on his shoulders, and told him, "Tell me what really happen."

Mohabir was so touched by Dularie's solicitude that tears came to his eyes. "So long I live in Canal, I never fight with anybody. Tonight, Dugdug and Snakeskin want to fight me and Baba."

"How Baba get mix up in this? Baba never drink and fight. He and Sita very religious. They go to *matya*[52] every Sunday."

"Baba only support me when I say that I gon tell the truth that Prashad been only joking, and Dugdug and Snakeskin raise up like ants' nest and want to fight us. Dugdug and Snakeskin hold on the front of our shirts and would'a hit us, but Papas came and stopped them."

Dularie had released Mohabir's hand a few moments earlier, and Mohabir made a motion to scratch his head, but his wife quicky restrained him again, and held them in her lap. Then she looked at her husband tenderly. "They want to behave like jackass. Let them. You don't sink to their level. Look how much people respect you in Canal. What about Slippery Ochro? Dugdug and Snakeskin are Slippery Ochro friends. Why didn't he stop them?"

"Slippery Ochro didn't say anything when they want to fight us, but when we coming home, he say that he would'a stop them if they want to hit us. I don't know why he didn't stop them at the beginning."

"We got to be careful with Slippery Ochro. Look how nice, nice we've been living before he build his house on our land. Since he move on our land, he cause nothing but trouble."

Mohabir reflected on this for a few minutes, and had to admit that it was true. Then he thought of Phulmattie on top of him, and remembered the soft feel of her breasts as they walked to Prashad. But the recency of Dugdug's and Snakeskin's assault dominated his thoughts, and he decided that the bad outweighed the good. Feeling that he had to respond to Dularie's observation, he said, "If we ask Slippery Ochro and Phulmattie to leave now, they gon cause more trouble for us."

---

[52] Hindu church

Dularie had to agree with Mohabir. "If we ask him to leave now, they gon take we to court and gon want us to give him our life savings to pay for the little house he build on our land. Slippery Ochro and Phulmattie gon make you spend the rest of your life in court for something or another. We don't want to spend our time like that in our old age. Wha *janjat*[53] we bring pon we head?"

Mohabir and Phulmattie sat quietly for a while, thinking about their situation, until they heard a knock on the back door. Both groaned and looked at each other, and both knew that it was either Slippery Ochro or Phulmattie, or both. Neither wanted to answer the door, but the knocking was persistent.

It's all my fault that all of this happened, Mohabir thought, as he got up to open the door. He was greeted by Phulmattie, her entire face contorted, and her eyes flashing. As she opened her mouth, her gold teeth caught the light from the kitchen lamp, sending sparks of fire.

She said, "I gon fix Dugdug and Snakeskin. Slippery Ochro tell me what happen. How you doing?"

Mohabir did not know how to answer, and started to scratch his head.

Dularie, who had gotten up and joined them by the door, answered for him. "Since I marry and came to Canal, Mohabir never get in a fight at the rum shop. Now, in his old age two hooligan want to beat him up. He very upset."

"I upset too. You all allow me and Slippery Ochro to build we house on your land, and we promised to look after you. We can buy rum for some of dem boys, give them some money, and let them beat they rass. Or we can take them to court. But we can't let them get away with this. What you want to do?"

Mohabir looked at Dularie. He did not consider himself a violent man, and earnestly did not wish to harm anybody, so the option of hiring some of the village thugs to beat Dugdug and Snakeskin did not exist for him. As for taking them to court, he hated going to court. He had already spent hours agonizing over going to court to give evidence in Slippery Ochro's case against Prashad.

Dularie answered for him. "We don't want to hurt anybody. If we pay some boys to beat up Dugdug and Snakeskin, then they and their friends

---

[53] Trouble

might beat up Mohabir. And we don't want to go to court. Mohabir worry every night about Slippery Ochro and Prashad case."

Phulmattie was puzzled. "What we gon do then?"

Both Mohabir and Dularie were stumped by this question. By nature, both were passive people, and they did not even consider that they were obliged to respond to the incident, but Phulmattie's question suggested otherwise. When Mohabir raised his hand to his head, Dularie again came to the rescue.

"Everything just happen so sudden. I gon give Mohabir something to eat, and then we gon go to sleep. We gon think what to do tomorrow," she told Phulmattie.

Dularie got up and started to dish out some food for Mohabir,

However, Phulmattie persisted. "Slippery Ochro and I gon come after breakfast tomorrow, and we gon talk about what to do. You can't let any Tom, Dick or Harry take advantage of you."

Dularie stopped putting rice on the plate she was preparing for Mohabir, and was furiously thinking of how to firmly tell Phulmattie that she did not want her to come with her husband in the morning, but it was not in her nature to be blunt.

Mohabir, on the other hand, was feeling the effects of the humiliating treatment by Dugdug and Snakeskin, and was becoming more and more convinced that something should be done about it. Although Slippery Ochro did not offer any support earlier in the evening, he was grateful for the support Phulmattie was demonstrating at that time.

"You right," he told Phulmattie. "I don't trouble anybody, and because I quiet, people think that they can take advantage of me. I don't know what to do about this situation, but you and Slippery Ochro got more experience about this sort of thing than me. You and Slippery Ochro come after breakfast tomorrow and we gon talk about what we gon do."

Phulmattie had noticed Dularie's hesitation a few moments earlier, and her gold teeth flashed triumphantly as she glanced at her. "Me and Slippery Ochro gon come in the morning. We na gon let anybody take advantage of you and get away with it. If we don't do anything now, they gon want to take advantage of you whenever they meet you, and you gon frighten to go and tekh a drink with your friends. Or even to go and buy groceries."

Dularie thought of her quiet, peace-loving husband being afraid to go out and have a drink, and was inclined to agree with Phulmattie. "We live in Canal before Dugdug and Snakeskin born. Now they want to make Mohabir frighten to go out and take a drink. You right. We got to put a stop to this. But how?"

"We gon talk about that tomorrow. I gon tell Slippery Ochro when I go home, and he can think about it. Don't worry. Slippery Ochro gon handle this situation. When he done with them, they *battie gon bite*[54] every time they see you. I gon go now, but I gon see you after breakfast tomorrow."

Phulmattie went to the door, but after two steps, she stopped and returned to the kitchen. "Or you want me and Slippery Ochro to come tomorrow and prepare breakfast for you. I pull out some cassava and eddoes from you farm yesterday, and we can come and cook boil and fry, and we all can have breakfast here. I know Mohabir like boil and fry."

As grateful as they were for Phulmattie's and Slippery Ochro's support, Mohabir and Dularie did not expect to have breakfast with them, although Mohabir was anxious to talk about what happened at Manbahal's rum shop with Slippery Ochro.

Phulmattie took their hesitation for agreement, and told them, "All right then. We gon come early tomorrow morning and prepare breakfast for you. Both of you can sleep in. We gon peel the provisions at home, so once you open the door for us, we can light the fire and put them to boil." With that, she turned and disappeared into the darkness, leaving Mohabir and Dularie looking at each other and wondering how Phulmattie managed to invite herself and her husband for breakfast.

"I hungry," Mohabir told his wife after a while.

Dularie got up, dished out some rice, dhal and fried fish, and placed it before him. Although he was indeed hungry, Mohabir was so disturbed by the evening's occurrences that he felt like he needed another drink before eating. He went to the kitchen, took out a bottle of El Dorado rum, and poured himself a large drink and some water.

As he drank, Dularie looked at him tenderly, thinking, *The husband I know is a hardworking man without a care in the world, except his farm. Now he wondering how he nearly get into a fight. I gon help him get through this, even if I got to side with Phulmattie.*

She started to feel better when Mohabir finished his drink and started eating. He was not usually a big eater, and Dularie was surprised when he

---

[54] They will be afraid

finished all the food on his plate. After he finished eating and brushing his teeth, she was even more surprised when he placed his hand tenderly around her waist, and gave a small squeeze.

"Let we go to bed," he said, as he exerted some pressure and led her to the bedroom. She willingly complied. After they made love, Dularie was very pleased when Mohabir promptly fell asleep. *It like old times*, she thought as she turned on her side and went to sleep.

Chapter 9

"Help that is not positively necessary is a hindrance to a growing organization."

—Dorothy Canfield Fisher—

At about two in the morning, Dularie was awakened by Mohabir thrashing, groaning and gnashing his teeth. When she shook him, he sat up, and she noticed that his face was covered with sweat. Dularie was worried—Mohabir was always a sound sleeper, She had witnessed this type of behavior when his mother died many years earlier.

She got up and got a towel to wipe the sweat off his face. "You had a bad dream," she told him. "What you dream about?"

"I dream that I was catching fish in a corial, and a huge caiman come under the boat and overturn it. Then when I fall overboard, it attack me. I climb on the boat, but it was leaping out of the water to get me. Then you wake me up."

"I wonder who is the caiman in we life?" Dularie asked, more of herself than of Mohabir.

"Slippery Ochro is more of a labaria than a caiman," Mohabir said. "He gon hide under a log, reach out and bite you and poison you, and pull back under the log. I can't go to sleep right away. I gon go to the kitchen and drink some water. Although I was in sweet water, I didn't have time to drink when the caiman was trying to eat me," he continued, attempting to joke as he got up from the bed.

Dularie lay in bed for a few minutes and then joined him in the kitchen. She expected to see him drinking water, but instead was surprised when she saw him with a bottle of El Dorado rum and a glass of water beside him. She remembered Mohabir getting up in the night and drinking on their wedding night, when they made love a number of times, and he took a drink after each session.

Although she knew that he was drinking because of what happened at Manbahal's rum shop, she asked him, "Why are you drinking in the night? You never used to wake up and drink."

"The dream made me frighten. I never had a dream like that before. And it seemed so real. I still don't know how I escape the caiman." He took another drink. "Now I scared to go in a canoe."

Dularie soothingly stroked her husband's arm and reassured him. "It because of everything that happened. Them young boys think that they own the world. They don't know you when you were young. Don't worry. Everything gon be over soon, and we can live our life peaceful again."

"You mean as soon as the court case with Prashad finish? Then we got to decide what to do with Dugdug and Snakeskin. I can't let them young boys drink rum and take them eyes pass me. I been working when they been running around in *shirt-tails*[55]. Older people than them respect me."

"We too soft to fight them. We not accustomed to dealing with people like them. They need somebody like..." Here Dularie paused for a few moments.

"Slippery Ochro," they both said in unison.

"Slippery Ochro and Phulmattie," Mohabir repeated. They gon come and cook breakfast, and then we gon talk about it."

"Yes," Dularie said. Although she was still conflicted about Slippery Ochro's and Phulmattie's involvement, she wanted Mohabir's mind to be at ease. "Leh we go to sleep now."

Mohabir said, "All right! Let me finish this drink first. You want a small drink to help you sleep?"

Dularie wanted a drink, but was fighting the temptation. *If I start waking up in the night and drink, what I gon turn to*, she thought. Aloud, she said, "All right, but just a small one. We can't make it a habit. Okay?"

Mohabir smiled at her mantra. "Okay!" He poured a drink for her and a little more rum for himself.

They finished their drinks, and went back to bed, Mohabir reached out to her to initiate a session of love making. Dularie was quite willing, but things were weighing so heavily on Mohabir's mind that he found himself unable to function.

Dularie threw her arms around him. "You still worried about them lungera. Don't worry about them. Leh we sleep."

---

[55] Without pants

Mohabir could not understand how two boys who grew up in front of his eyes would want to fight him, and how he had reached the stage when he was thinking of planning of ways to punish those boys with Slippery Ochro and Phulmattie. However, the drinks he had consumed had a somnolent effect, and he soon drifted off to sleep, his wife arms still around his shoulder.

It seemed as if they had just closed their eyes when Mohabir and Dularie heard a knocking on their kitchen door. Dularie, still solicitous of Mohabir, decided that she would be the one to get up. She put on a sweater and opened the kitchen door—not surprised to see Slippery Ochro and Phulmattie outside. Phulmattie had on an orange and white headscarf and had an aluminum bowl filled with peeled provisions, cut into small pieces, while Slippery Ochro was dressed in a black serge trousers and a plaid shirt. Both were barefoot..

Phulmattie, gold teeth flashing, greeted her. "Eh, eh, girl, like we wake you up."

"Mohabir and I didn't sleep well last night. He still in bed." Dularie contemplated telling Phulmattie why she and Mohabir didn't sleep well, but decided against it.

"He worried about what Dugdug and Snakeskin did," Slippery Ochro said as he made his way into the kitchen and went to the fireside to light the fire. "Don't worry. When Mohabir wake up, we gon plan how to fix them," he reassured Dularie as he poured kerosene over some kindling and got the fire started.

Phulmattie started washing the provisions in the sink.

Dularie felt so useless in her own kitchen that she made her way to the cupboard where the pots were kept, and took out a large pot, filled it with water, and put it on the fireside. By this time, Mohabir had joined them, eyes half closed, and wearing the same clothes he had worn the previous night.

The fire was going strong by then, and Slippery Ochro decided to leave the women to do the rest. He put his arm around Mohabir's shoulder and reassured him. "Dularie tell me and Phulmattie that both of you didn't sleep well last night. I know it was because of what Dugdug and Snakeskin did. A respected man like you should not have to put up with things like that. We gon fix them. We gon talk about what we gon do after we drink coffee and have breakfast."

Mohabir sat at the table. Slippery Ochro followed, his hand still around Mohabir's shoulder.

Phulmattie put the water on to boil for the coffee, and Dularie took out the ground coffee from the cupboard and placed it on the counter. Mohabir and Slippery Ochro looked at each other. Both wanted to broach the topic of the two young men accosting Mohabir, but decided to wait until after breakfast.

Mohabir was so troubled about Slippery Ochro's lack of support the previous evening that he could wait no longer and said, "Slippery Ochro, why you didn't ask them boys to stop last night? They your friends."

Slippery Ochro looked at Mohabir, then at Dularie, before he focused his gaze on Phulmattie, who understood his plea for help, and answered for her husband. "Slippery Ochro not really friends with Dugdug and Snakeskin. They only know each other. But he want to be friends with you and Dularie."

Mohabir was pleasantly surprised when Dularie, normally a soft-spoken woman, and who avoided conflict at all costs, told Phulmattie, "You mean he like a razor blade? He cut from both sides." Both Slippery Ochro and Phulmattie were equally surprised, and were silent for a long period.

Phulmattie again came to the rescue. "You know how people in Canal stay. Sometimes, you got to cut from both sides if you want to live. We gon cut anybody from all sides if they think that they can *eye-pass*[56] Mohabir."

She looked at Mohabir and Dularie and noticed them relaxing visibly. This gave her courage to continue. "As for Snakeskin and Dugdug, they gon get what coming to them." She looked at Slippery Ochro, who took her cue.

"You too respectable to be involved in a fight, or even to pay some people to beat them up. I don't want you to be involved in that. The best thing is to take them to court. I gon take you to Haynes today. You know that he already handling my case with Prashad. I gon ask him for a discount for your case. Or we can ask him not to charge us, and take a percentage of whatever money you get from Dugdug and Snakeskin. I been friends with them, but we not friends anymore, after what they did to you."

Slippery Ochro did not wait for an answer, but turned his attention to his wife. "Phulmattie, take out some coffee for me and Mohabir. We gon drink it while we wait for the boil and fry." He turned to Mohabir. "We

---

[56] Show disrespect

gon *fix their backsides*[57]. We gon hit them where it hurts. You know that they not working. If we take them to court, where they gon find the money from to hire a lawyer. You got the money, so you can hire Haynes, and we gon win for sure. What you think, Dularie? You want your husband to fight Dugdug and Snakeskin, or take them to court?"

Dularie did not have time to consider whether there were other possibilities. Out of the two alternatives, the choice was obvious. "Even when Mohabir young, he didn't like to fight. Now when he old, I don't want him to get involved in any fight. But Snakeskin and Dugdug don't have any money to give Mohabir as compensation. And we not short of money. All we want is for them to stop picking fight with Mohabir."

Dularie looked at Mohabir, who looked at Slippery Ochro. Slippery Ochro awarded them one of his sly smiles as he told Mohabir, "We got to listen to what the women saying sometimes. They only want to keep we out of trouble. We got to stop Dugdug and Snakeskin from taking advantage of Mohabir because he so soft."

Mohabir was surprised when Dularie reinforced Slippery Ochro's statement. "I don't want you to get into any fight at your age," Dularie told her husband. "Look when Bhagdan killed he neighbor, Seedan, over one coffee tree. The coffee tree been on the surveyor line, and they argue about who should pick the coffee from the tree. They drink and fight, and Bhagdan chop up Seedan. Now Seedan can't pick coffee from the tree because he dead, and Bhagdan can't pick coffee from the tree because he in jail. When dem boy drink, they don't know what they do. I don't want you to get involved in that."

Mohabir shuddered when he remembered Seedan being put in a *corial*[58], because the rains had made the mud road unusable by cars. Seedan bled out before he reached Dr. Singh at Good Fortuin, and the police came in their four-wheel drive land rover to arrest Bhagdan the following day. He thought that if Dugdug and Snakeskin had a cutlass at Manbahal's the previous night, they would have chopped him. "Leh we go and see Haynes after breakfast," he told Slippery Ochro. When he glanced at Dularie, he saw her nodding her head, and felt better,

Slippery Ochro smiled, while Phulmattie redoubled her efforts to prepare breakfast, both obviously ecstatic about how events unfolded.

---

[57] Reek some sort of vengeance
[58] A dugout canoe

After breakfast, Slippery Ochro got up and told Mohabir, "I gon go and get ready now. It's too late to catch the nine o'clock boat, but we can get the eleven o'clock boat."

Mohabir was having second thoughts about the whole enterprise and wanted to buy some time. "How about if we go tomorrow?" However, there was a certain tentativeness in his voice which was immediately detected by Slippery Ochro.

"It better to do these things right away," Slippery Ochro replied. "You never know if Haynes take on a big case today, and when we go tomorrow, he tell us that he too busy. I gon go and get ready and I gon come back to pick you up in about half an hour. Phulmattie, you help Dularie clean up while I go and change."

Mohabir resented Slippery Ochro giving orders in his house, but rationalized that Slippery Ochro was ordering his own wife. As soon as Slippery Ochro left, he went in his room, and put on a pair of his grey all-wool trousers and a clean and ironed white shirt, and walked in the kitchen just as Slippery Ochro came to get him. Slippery Ochro was dressed in starched and ironed khaki trousers and a checkered shirt. The felt hat of an unknown brand which Slippery Ochro was wearing had seen better days, and the brim was floppy and looked as if it was going to cover his ears. Mohabir's Wilson hat was shaped and firm around the crown, and had a multicolored feather in its hatband..

They met in the kitchen. Phulmattie looked at both men and felt a tinge of jealousy. "When you get your settlement from Prashad, you must buy a hat like Mohabir's," she told Slippery Ochro.

Dularie reflected on the exchange and thought, *They ask us to build a small house on our land, and now they jealous of what we got.* She turned to Mohabir and said, "Make sure you take enough money for lunch, because you might finish too late to come back home for lunch."

"We gon go to one of the cookshop in Stabroek Market and eat lunch there after we finish with Haynes. Let we go and try and get a hire car, Slippery Ochro," Mohabir responded, as he and Slippery Ochro walked down the kitchen stairs and headed to Gobin bridge to get a hire car, leaving Phulmattie and Dularie in the kitchen.

"Mohabir looked nice," Phulmattie told Dularie. "I wish Slippery Ochro tekh care of himself like Mohabir."

Dularie did not know how to respond, and was silent for quite a few moments thinking, *How she comparing Slippery Ochro with Mohabir. What should I tell her?* "Mohabir start working when he been fourteen," she told Phulmattie. "Even when he left Wales office, he work hard on the farm. And he never smoke. Except when he go to weddings, Mohabir didn't drink much. We take a drink or two before dinner. The most drinking we did in our lives was since you and Slippery Ochro build your house on our land." As soon she said it, Dularie knew that it was the wrong thing to say, and the look on Phulmattie's face confirmed it.

"You mean me and Slippery Ochro cause you and Mohabir to drink? We never force you to drink."

Dularie knew where the conversation was heading and didn't want a confrontation with Phulmattie. "I mean that we didn't have company to drink, before. It better to drink with company."

Phulmattie relaxed. "Slippery Ochro like to go to the rum shop and drink with his friends sometimes, and I take a drink or two with him at home. But we didn't have friends like you and Mohabir to drink with. Me and you can't go to the rum shop, or else people gon talk. One time I tell Slippery Ochro that I gon go with him to Manbahal shop when he been meeting with my cousin, Kawall, and he ask me if I was a man. He say that only men go to the rum shop. Like women don't have mouth to drink with too?"

Dularie had no desire to drink at the rum shop, and accepted that only men went to drink there, but she thought about what Phulmattie said, and changed the topic. "I hope that things go well with Haynes and Mohabir and Slippery Ochro today."

"Don't worry! Haynes knows Slippery Ochro well. He handle a lot of cases for us. Everything gon be all right."

This was not news to Dularie, because she was only too well aware of Slippery Ochro's and Phulmattie's exploits with the courts. However, she was happy to have the couple on her side on this occasion.

**

Mohabir and Slippery Ochro got in Manick's hire car to get the eleven o'clock ferry from Vreedenhoop to Georgetown. By that time, everybody in Canal knew that Slippery Ochro had built his house on Mohabir's land, but Manick considered that it was unlikely that the two would have business in Georgetown together. "You going to town together?" Manick asked.

Mohabir did not know what to say and kept quiet. Slippery Ochro, on the other hand, was reveling in his new-found relationship with Mohabir. "You know them good-for-nothing lungera, Dugdug and Snakeskin, want to beat up Mohabir last night? They drink one cent rum, and play a dollar drunk. They got nothing to lose when they get drunk and fight, but Mohabir is a respected man in Canal. He got a lot to lose. We gon see Haynes to sue them ass."

Slippery Ochro knew full well that it was only a matter of time before that particular bit of news would be transmitted to the whole of Canal.

"But you and Dugdug and Snakeskin are buddies?"

"We friends until they take their eyes pass Mohabir. Mohabir allow me to build me house on his land, and to pick orange and tangerine from his trees. I not going to let anybody take advantage of him."

Mohabir said, "You know, Manick, them young boys want to take advantage of me at my age. I won't degrade myself to fight them, but I can't let them take advantage of me. The only thing I can do is take them to court."

"Them young boys these days don't have no respect for anybody," Manick said. "Somebody got to teach them to have respect. So, what you gon do? Sue them? They don't have any money you can sue them for."

Slippery Ochro told Manick, "I tell Mohabir that not to sue them for money. Just let the judge fine their ass."

"They won't have any money to pay any fine. They gon have to go to jail," Manick reminded Slippery Ochro.

"It good if they go to jail," Slippery Ochro replied. "They can't get rum in jail, and drink and get drunk and want to beat up people. Jail got plenty bad people."

Manick was very proud of Canal, and liked the residents with all their eccentricities. He did not want anybody from Canal going to jail. "But they didn't beat up Mohabir. They just get drunk and shoot their mouth off. Plenty people drunk and say things they don't mean."

"Many times, people drink and say things that been on their minds for a long time," Slippery Ochro countered. "Dugdug and Snakeskin always jealous of Mohabir. Then they get drunk, or pretend to get drunk, and want to beat him up. If Papas wouldn'a come in, God only knows what would'a happen."

Manick said, "Mohabir, you belong to the Panchayat in Canal. You know how everybody respect you. You really want to send two Canal man to jail?"

Mohabir scratched his head vigorously as he reflected upon his position in the village, and on the number of disputes which he adjudicated and resolved. In all of the instances, the parties involved had accepted the decision of the Panchayat, and the police and the court system had no need to be involved. He was about to tell Manick to drop them off, so that they could return home.

Slippery Ochro interrupted. "You know that Mohabir and Dularie didn't sleep last night because of what Dugdug and Snakeskin did. Manick, you're right. Mohabir is a respected man in the village, and people can't feel that they can drink rum and threaten to beat him up, so that he and his wife can't sleep. People like that don't belong in Canal. Besides, Snakeskin and Dugdug got no respect for Panchayat, and won't listen to the people in the Panchayat."

Mohabir thought of the trouble he and Dularie had sleeping the previous night, and thought that Slippery Ochro was right. After all, he didn't trouble anybody, and should not be subjected to the treatment that Dugdug and Snakeskin had given him. "Sometimes, people who *hard ears* have to learn the hard way," he told Manick. "I like the people in Canal, but we can't let one or two people spoil everything. You say that Dugdug and Snakeskin don't have money. Where they get money to buy rum from?"

Then he remembered that it was Slippery Ochro and Baba who bought the rum for Dugdug and Snakeskin, but stayed quiet.

Manick was silent for a few minutes, and welcomed the distraction when he had to stop and pick up Fat Finey, who had flagged him down. The polka dot dress she wore could hardly contain her body which overflowed from it on the neck, arms, hips, and everywhere. People did not really know how she had gotten the name *Finey*, because that was her name when she got married and came to the village. She could have been described as pretty when she arrived in her bridal outfit, but afterwards she ballooned to over two hundred and eighty pounds.

People did not call her *Fat Finey* to be cruel, but for purposes of identification, because there were two other women in the village named *Finey*, and people had to distinguish between them. The two others were known as *Black Tongue Finey*, because everything she said turned out to be true, and *Short Finey*, for obvious reasons.

Manick opened the front door for Fat Finey, knowing full well that he could not seat any other passengers in the front seat. He would collect only a single fare from her, although some of the other hire car drivers demanded that she pay two fares. The debate about whether Mohabir was doing the right thing ceased with Fat Finey's entrance in the car, partly because Manick and Mohabir did not feel comfortable discussing the issue with anybody else, but mostly because Fat Finey dominated the conversation as soon as she seated herself.

"Manick, thank you for giving me the whole of the front seat. You know that jackass, Budya, always make me pay two fares. If he want to starve his wife, that his business. Heh, eh, Mohabir, I didn't see you for a long time. Where you going?" Fat Finey didn't wait for an answer, but addressed Slippery Ochro. "Slippery Ochro, you got another court case? Which court you going to? Wales or Georgetown?"

"Why you think that every time I go out, I going to court? I going with Mohabir. Dugdug and Snakeskin want to beat him up last night, and we going to see Haynes." As he was saying it, Slippery Ochro got a flash of insight, and turning to Mohabir, told him, "You don't have to ask the judge to fine Dugdug and Snakeskin, and they don't have to go to jail if they don't pay the fine. We gon ask Haynes to get a restraining order—"

Fat Finey asked, "What is a restraining order?"

"A restraining order mean that they can't bring their backsides closer than five hundred yards to Mohabir. When I been to Wales court one time, a man was beating his ex-wife, and the magistrate put a restraining order on him. If he go within five hundred yards of his wife, they gon put his backside in jail."

Mohabir breathed a sigh of relief. In spite of what he was saying about justice, he was agonizing about putting a resident of Canal in jail, and accepted Slippery Ochro's suggestion readily. "That the best thing, Slippery Ochro. What you think, Manick?"

Before Manick could answer, Fat Finey volunteered her opinion, "Mohabir gon get bad, bad name if he put anybody in Canal in jail. And what gon happen when Dugdug and Snakeskin come out of jail? The restraining order is the best thing. Do the restraining order thing, Mohabir."

"Fat Finey right," Manick said as he took his eyes off the road and turned briefly to Mohabir in the back seat. "We all Canal people together and we don't want to put each other in jail."

Although he had suggested the restraining order alternative, things were going too smoothly for Slippery Ochro and he decided to put a spanner in the works. "My house more than five hundred yard from yours. That means that I can invite Dugdug and Snakeskin for a drink if I want."

Fat Finey said, "You build your house on Mohabir land. Now you're saying that Mohabir can't come near your house on his own land. Why Dugdug and Snakeskin got to come to your house?"

"I have my home there. I speak to Haynes, and he say that a man's home is his castle, even though he build it on somebody else land." Inspired by a burst of confidence, Slippery Ochro added, "You know that I can put Mohabir out from my home, although it on his land?"

Mohabir resumed scratching his head, as Fat Finey asked Slippery Ochro, "You mean that you can put Mohabir out from his own land?"

"No! I can't put him out from his own land, but I can put him out from my house, although I build it on his land. But I can't put him out from anybody else house. Balgobin had a quarrel with his sister-in-law, Sandra, and she promise to put him out of any of her brother houses. Legally, she got no right to do that, except if her brothers give her permission. Balgobin know how *besharam*[59] Sandra is, so he stop going to any of his brother-in-law homes for a while."

Fat Finey continued her interrogation of Slippery Ochro, "What about Mohabir land around your house? He can't go there, too?"

"He can't come too close to my house. My walls got a lot of creases. I don't want him to peep me and Phulmattie."

Although Fat Finey didn't know Mohabir well, she ventured, "I don't think that Mohabir is a *Peep Man*."

Mohabir felt completely left out of the conversation as Manick interrupted. "I don't think that Mohabir is a Peep Man, either, but you can't tell with people these days. Look at Saroop. He married and live with his wife and had three children, and then he left she and went to live with another man in Georgetown."

Mohabir squirmed and started scratching his head until Slippery Ochro noticed blood under his fingernails, and decided to do some serious backtracking. "I don't know why you all talking about Peep Man and

---

[59] Shameless

Saroop. Mohabir is a good man, and he allow me to build my house on his land. I just talking about the law."

Manick had previously refused to stop for three passengers because the conversation was going so sweet that he did not want to interrupt it, but since it became somewhat dull, he stopped for Lam, a surveyor, who made frequent trips to Georgetown. Lam was a slim man, and was dressed in a grey serge trousers, white shirt and red tie. Never mind how warm the weather was, Lam always wore a tie, and was known as being very polite, but formal, speaking only when necessary and using as few words as possible. It was not surprising that the tone of the conversation changed as soon as he entered the car.

"Morning Mr. Lam," Manick greeted as he opened the back door. Mohabir, who had stopped scratching his head, was now sandwiched between Lam and Slippery Ochro.

"Morning," Lam replied.

Slippery Ochro wanted to continue sharing his views, but recognizing the fact that Lam's response did not leave room for further conversation, stayed quiet. So did Mohabir and Fat Finey, until they reached Vreedenhoop where they hurried to buy tickets for the eleven o'clock ferry.

**

They disembarked at Georgetown and Slippery Ochro led Mohabir straight to Haynes' office in Croal Street. After walking for a while, the air-conditioned office felt good to Mohabir, although he was a bit nervous as he glanced at the three people in the waiting room.

I wonder what kind of problem they got, Mohabir thought, as Slippery Ochro went straight to the receptionist.

"Hello, George, I forget to bring some oranges for you. I gon l bring some next time."

He talking about my oranges, Mohabir said to himself.

Slippery Ochro continued, "I bring my friend, Mohabir to see Mr. Haynes. Two rum suckers from Canal threatened to beat him up."

"Okay, Slippery Ochro! Have a seat, and Mr. Haynes will see you and your friend shortly."

Slippery Ochro and Mohabir sat in the last vacant seats in the small waiting room. "George is also a notary public, and can write an affidavit and witness you sign it," Slippery Ochro told Mohabir in a tone loud enough for George to hear.

"The last time I go to a lawyer office was when I bought my house and land, and had to have the deed transferred to my name," Mohabir whispered.

Slippery Ochro, again in a tone which carried to George, replied, "It good to know a good lawyer. People can't take advantage of you. They respect you."

You mean that they're scared of you, Mohabir thought.

After a while, the door to Haynes' office opened and a tall portly gentleman, with a generous crop of silver hair, walked into the waiting room. His striped, black suit, clean white shirt, blue tie, and shoes polished to a military shine were meant to inspire confidence in his clients. And they did. All the people in the waiting room, including Mohabir, got up as Haynes approached George. "Mr. Alleyne will give you a retainer, and I will represent him in this case. Then we have to wait for a court date. Who's next?"

A man, and a woman, stood up and followed Haynes into his office, leaving Slippery Ochro and Mohabir feeling relaxed, knowing that there was only one person ahead of them.

After about half an hour, Haynes called Slippery Ochro and Mohabir into his office, and addressed Slippery Ochro, "How are you, Slippery Ochro?"

"I am fine, Mr. Haynes. Two drunken young men threaten to beat up my friend, Mohabir. He allow me to build my house on his land. We were going sue to them, but we know that they don't have any money, and Mohabir say that he just want a restraining order. He want them to stay away from him."

"A restraining order is a good first step," Haynes said "If they don't follow the restraining order, then we will have a stronger case against them. It is also less expensive than a court case. It will cost your friend only one hundred dollars."

Mohabir realized that he was being left out of the conversation but did not mind. He was intimidated by the environment and felt that he could not present his case as effectively as Slippery Ochro. He admired how effortlessly Slippery Ochro spoke with Haynes and envied his confidence in this setting.

Without consulting Mohabir, Slippery Ochro told Haynes, "All right! We gon pay the one hundred dollars for the restraining order."

"I will have George draw up a request for a restraining order to be presented to the judge. Your friend can pay him. Give him the legal name of your friend and the names of the people you want the restraining order against."

Slippery Ochro looked at Mohabir, and Mohabir looked at Slippery Ochro. They both said in unison, "Dugdug and Snakeskin."

Haynes laughed loudly. "We can't type a restraining order against Dugdug and Snakeskin. You have to give me their legal names."

"We only know them as Dugdug and Snakeskin," Slippery Ochro said.

"You have to go back home, find out their names, and come back. "You still have to leave a retainer. George will prepare the affidavit and leave the names blank for now."

Mohabir mustered all his courage to ask Slippery Ochro, "What's a retainer?"

"It mean you got to pay him," Slippery Ochro replied.

Why didn't he just say so? Mohabir thought. *Why did he have to use all the fancy words?*

As soon as they exited Haynes' office, Mohabir peeled one hundred dollars from the roll of bills in his pocket, gave it to Slippery Ochro, and admired the easy manner with which Slippery Ochro chatted with the legal assistant as he passed over the money.

"The village office will have the right names of Dugdug and Snakeskin," Slippery Ochro told George. "We will get them and come back the day after tomorrow."

Haynes was already leading the next client into his office as Slippery Ochro and Mohabir left the reception area. The air outside felt unduly warm after time spent in the air-conditioned office, as they decided to forego lunch, and hurried to catch the two o'clock ferry.

Slippery Ochro told Mohabir, "I gon go to Suruj Bali and get the right names. He is the overseer and he got the right names of all the people in the village. We can come back tomorrow, but I already tell George that we gon come back day after tomorrow. We gon pick some oranges and tangerines for George when we go back to see Haynes. We never know when we gon ask him a favor. It good to keep close with all these legal people."

This time, Mohabir did not mind that Slippery Ochro was giving away his oranges and tangerines as if they were his, and felt grateful for his support.

As Mohabir lined up to buy tickets for himself and Slippery Ochro for the two o'clock ferry, he told Slippery Ochro, "We gon be home about three o'clock, and we can eat lunch at home. I gon drop in at Manbahal and buy a bottle of Russian Bear, so that we can have a few drinks before we eat,"

In response, Slippery Ochro awarded him one of his sly smiles.

Manick was soliciting passengers when the ferry arrived at Vreedenhoop, and he approached them,

Slippery Ochro, cautioned him, "We gon come in your car, Manick, but we don't want to talk about our case with the other passengers. We don't want the whole of Canal to know about our business," knowing full well that Manick would tell everybody in Canal about the impending court case.

"You're right," Manick replied. "Many people in Canal walk with their mouth. We won't talk about the case in the car."

The car had five passengers when Slippery Ochro and Mohabir squeezed in, and one seven-year-old boy had to sit on Mohabir's lap. Manick felt he had a full load and went behind the driver's wheel. Next to him was a divorced woman who had moved back in with her parents when her husband indicated that he did not want her anymore. People in Canal unkindly called her *Top-Heavy Leila* because of her large breasts. Mohabir smiled as Manick used the slightest excuse to change gears, rubbing his elbows against Leila's prominent breasts. Leila did not seem to mind, as she flushed and smiled at Manick.

Manick should not charge her for this trip. He should pay her instead, Mohabir thought.

Manick's elbow was still working overtime when Slippery Ochro asked him to stop outside the village office in Canal so that he could speak with Suruj Bali.

"I gon buy a bottle at Manbahal and take it home," Mohabir told Slippery Ochro as he exited the car. "When you finish with Suruj Bali, come straight to my house. We gon take one or two before we eat lunch."

"Okay. I gon come to your place as soon as I get the right names," Slippery Ochro replied.

Top Heavy Leila asked, "Who right name you looking for?" Then Slippery Ochro remembered that he wasn't supposed to talk about the case,

Although some passengers had already been dropped off at their homes, and there was ample space in the front seat, she was still seated very close to Manick, allowing his elbow easy access to her breasts.

Both Slippery Ochro and Mohabir were stumped, not wanting to tell everybody in the car about their case.

Feeling that he had no alternative, Mohabir blurted out, "Snakeskin and Dugdug."

One of the passengers, Bhai Bhai, who was unaware of the case, told Mohabir and Slippery Ochro, "You don't need their right names. Everybody know them. You can ask the smallest boy or girl where Snakeskin and Dugdug live, and they gon tell you."

"They threaten to beat up Mohabir, and we gon sue they ass," Slippery Ochro blurted out. Then he remembered their conversation with Haynes. "Or at least we gon get a restraining order so that they can't come within five hundred yards of Mohabir. But Haynes need they right name to draw up the restraining order. People in Canal know Snakeskin and Dugdug, but the lawyers and the judge won't know them."

Bhai Bhai, a plump gentleman with a friendly face and a perpetual smile, who was an elder in the village, turned to Mohabir and said, "Mohabir, you and me belong to the Panchayat. Let the Panchayat meet with Snakeskin and Dugdug, and we can tell them to stop bothering you. No need to meet with lawyers. People don't call them *liars* for nothing. We don't need them to help us deal with any problems in Canal."

Mohabir felt very contrite at being chastised by another member of the Panchayat and was on the verge of accepting Bhai Bhai's suggestion.

Slippery Ochro piped in: "Where the Panchayat been when Charlie chop up Sugrim with his axe? Where the Panchayat been when Gola poison her husband? Where the Panchayat been when Dugdug and Snakeskin nearly beat up Mohabir?"

Slippery Ochro's outburst gave Mohabir time to think of a more diplomatic reply, and he responded to Bhai Bhai. "You and me belong to the Panchayat, and I don't want everybody to think that I using the

Panchayat to settle my personal quarrels, especially when this one happen in a rum shop."

Bhai Bhai agreed. "It don't look good for a member of the Panchayat to be involved in a rum shop fight. You always been a quiet and respectable man, Mohabir. How come you end up fighting in the rum shop?"

Slippery Ochro came to Mohabir's rescue. "It not Mohabir fault. Mohabir been taking a nice quiet drink with me when Dugdug and Snakeskin start on him. Prashad tell Mohabir that it look like he take a second wife when Phulmattie went with him to buy a bottle of rum. You cannot blame Mohabir because of what Prashad tell him. It Prashad's mouth, not Mohabir mouth that the words came from. The whole of Canal know that I suing Prashad backside for slander. And I gon sue anybody who bad mouth me or Mohabir."

This was enough to convince everybody in the car to keep their mouths shut, as Slippery Ochro went to the village office and Manick put the car in gear.

Mohabir, emotionally worn out by the day's activities, badly needed a drink, and asked Manick to drop him off at Manbahal's rum shop where he bought a bottle of Russian Bear and headed home.

Chapter 10

A name represents identity, a deep feeling and holds tremendous significance to its owner.

—Rachel Ingber—

Dularie was washing clothes at the standpipe when Mohabir walked across the bridge spanning the four-foot drain in front of the house. She turned off the tap as he approached. "Mohabir, you come back early. Everything go okay?"

"We see Haynes, and we ask him to put a restraining order on Snakeskin and Dugdug, but he couldn't do it because we didn't have their right names. Slippery Ochro stop off at the village office to see Suruj Bali and get their right names. We gon go back and see Haynes the day after tomorrow."

Dularie laughed out loud. "We know everybody by their call-names. We don't need their right names, but the lawyer gon need their right names. We should'a think of that."

"Slippery Ochro gon get their right names and will give me after he see Suruj Bali."

Dularie could not help but emphasize to Mohabir, "Slippery Ochro put we in this situation in the first place."

"You know that Slippery Ochro can stop us from going near his house?" Mohabir asked his wife.

"I know that we can't go in his house, although it on our land," Dularie replied. "But it our land, and we can go on our land."

"Yes, but how close can we go to he house?"

"I don't know how close. Why you want to go close to Slippery Ochro and Phulmattie house for?"

The fact that Dularie included Phulmattie was not lost on Mohabir. "I don't want to go close to Slippery Ochro and Phulmattie house. I just want to know where I can go on me own land."

When Mohabir started to scratch his head, Dularie quickly added, "But at least they helping we to fix our problem with Dugdug and Snakeskin."

Mohabir raised the bottle of Russian Bear in his hand. "I buy a bottle of rum to have a drink with Slippery Ochro, before lunch. After all, he spend the whole day with me. You prepare lunch?"

"You say that you gon eat lunch in one of the cook shop."

"Yes, but we finish so fast at Haynes, that I say we gon come home and have a drink or two and eat at home."

"I got some dholl and rice, and I gon fry up some eggs quick, quick for you all, but lemme[60] finish washing these two piece clothes."

Before she resumed washing the clothes, she queried Mohabir, "But why you buy a large bottle of rum?" Then she demonstrated her displeasure by sitting down wordlessly, resuming her washing, while Mohabir went upstairs to change from his going-out clothes to his house-clothes.

After about half an hour, there was a knock on the front door, and when Mohabir opened it, he saw Slippery Ochro triumphantly waving a piece of paper. "I got they name. I didn't go home yet. I come straight here," he said with a wide smile, handing Mohabir the paper with the names: *'Ram Ramlogan and Sugrim Bridgemohan.*

"Which one is Dugdug and which one is Snakeskin?" Mohabir asked, and saw a blank stare on Slippery Ochro's face.

"Suruj Bali write the name down and give the paper to me," he replied softly. Then he thought about the situation some more and reassured Mohabir, "We don't have to know which one is which. We gon file a restraining order on both of them."

Mohabir was visibly relieved until Dularie, who left the kitchen to join them, asked, "But who you gon serve the restraining order to? Suppose you give Dugdug Snakeskin restraining order and you give Snakeskin Dugdug restraining order. What gon happen then?"

Mohabir and Slippery Ochro looked at each other then at Dularie, as if she was the problem.

Slippery Ochro said, "I gon go back to Suruj Bali tomorrow and let him tell me which name belong to who." Then he remembered that Mohabir

---

[60] Let me

said that he would buy a bottle of rum, and looked at him expectantly. "Or I can go today, after we take a few, and eat a bit."

Mohabir took the hint, and said, "Dularie prepare lunch for us. I buy a bottle of Russian Bear. Leh we take a few, and then we gon eat."

"All right! But let me go home first and tell Phulmattie that I come home. I might ask her to come over and take a drink with us."

Now, it was Mohabir's and Dularie turn to look at each other, but neither said anything as Slippery Ochro walked down the stairs with the paper he had retrieved from Mohabir.

In about ten minutes, Slippery Ochro returned, Phulmattie in tow, her gold teeth flashing expectantly in the sun.

Phulmattie said, "Slippery Ochro tell me that he got the two right name from Suruj Bali, but Suruj Bali didn't tell him which name belong to who. Never mind, Slippery Ochro can go back tomorrow, and Suruj Bali gon tell him which name belong to which lungera."

Slippery Ochro ignored his wife's teasing, and asked Mohabir, "You buy Russian Bear or El Dorado?" This, of course, was another way of reminding him to bring the rum.

Mohabir turned to Dularie. "You gon bring the glasses and cola, and I gon get the Russian Bear. Leh we take everything downstairs. It got more breeze downstairs."

"I gon help you," Phulmattie told Dularie, and they both headed to the kitchen while Mohabir went for the rum.

The four settled under the house and Mohabir handed the full bottle to Slippery Ochro. "You open it and check under the cork for a Russian Bear picture. "

Slippery Ochro open the bottle, looked at the cork, and shook his head in disappointment, before throwing a few drops on the ground and pouring for himself and passing the bottle to Mohabir. After a few drinks, they all felt mellow, and both Slippery Ochro and Mohabir felt better about not remembering to take the right names of Dugdug and Snakeskin to Haynes.

After downing his fourth drink and putting his glass on the coffee table, Slippery Ochro turned to Mohabir and Dularie with a cunning smile. "If people want to sue me, and they sue Slippery Ochro, that not my right name, so I don't got to go to court."

"What your right name?" Mohabir asked.

"That for me to know and for you to guess," Slippery Ochro replied.

"I, too, can go to Suruj Bali and get your right name," Mohabir said.

"Only if you want to take me to court," Slippery Ochro continued as he poured another drink.

Mohabir turned to Slippery Ochro. "I gon eat after this drink. You hungry?"

"I been hungry since we take the ferry to come to Vreedenhoop."

Dularie went to the kitchen, with Phulmattie in her trail, leaving their husbands with their drinks.

Phulmattie said, "Girl, I didn't eat lunch either. I been waiting on Slippery Ochro."

Dularie was not worried about having to feed another person. Like most people in Canal, and indeed, in the country areas, she cooked a lot of rice, and more than enough curry for herself and Mohabir. Phulmattie eating with them would mean there would be less curry to flavor the rice, but everyone would eat his or her fill, albeit with carbohydrates. The two women dished out rice and apportioned the curry to the four plates, before taking the plates to the bottom-house.

As they ate, they continued joking about the day's events.

"You should see Haynes' face when we asked him to file a restraining order against Snakeskin and Dugdug," Slippery Ochro told the group, as he slapped his thighs with both his arms.

"And when you ask Suruj Bali for their right names, he just give you two right name. He didn't tell you which is which," Mohabir reminded Slippery Ochro.

At this point, he decided to acknowledge Dularie's contribution. "And if it wasn't for Dularie, we would'a gone to Haynes and asked him to do two restraining orders, without knowing who to give which restraining order to." Both men slapped their knees, and roared with laughter.

The two men ate ravenously, their appetites whetted by the late hour and the drinks, while the women, mindful of the predicament their husbands were in, supported them, each in her unique way.

Dularie told her husband, "Don't worry, Mohabir. Everything gon be okay. Haynes gon get the restraining order, and those two drunken louts na gon[61] bother you again."

Phulmattie, on the other hand, stroked Slippery Ochro's ego, as she encouraged him. "You give them good, Slippery Ochro. Show them that they can't take their eyes pass you or Mohabir. Whether we poor or rich, we human being just like everybody else."

Slippery Ochro looked at her lovingly, and awarded her his sly smile.

By the time lunch was finished, so was the bottle, and Mohabir and Dularie went upstairs to a well-deserved nap, while Slippery Ochro and Phulmattie went through the coffee trees to their house.

Once they were upstairs, Dularie put her hand on her husband's arm and tenderly told him, "I sorry that you got mixed up in all of this. You not accustomed to all of this court business."

Mohabir put his arm around his wife. "Me too. I don't want to get involved, but Slippery Ochro right. If I don't do something, Dugdug and Snakeskin gon want to pick a fight with me whenever they see me. I live in Canal so long, and I never frighten to go and take a drink at the rum shop. I don't want to start now."

Dularie thought of her peace-loving, helpful husband, whom everybody loved and respected, and hugged Mohabir tighter. "You right. You old enough to be Dugdug and Snakeskin father. And this is the respect they show you? Leh we go and rest now."

**

The following morning while they were having breakfast, Dularie and Mohabir heard a knocking at the kitchen door and looked at each other with exasperation. After spending almost all of the previous day with Slippery Ochro or Phulmattie, or both, they felt a need to be alone for a while. Nevertheless, with his mouth full of roti and boulangers, Mohabir opened the door to find Slippery Ochro standing on the other side with a handful of tangerines.

"I know how much Dularie like these tangerines. I say I gon pick some for her," he said as he peered into the kitchen. As Mohabir accepted the tangerines picked from his own tree, Slippery Ochro continued, "You all having breakfast? I didn't have breakfast yet you know."

---

[61] Not going to

Mohabir knew that it was extremely bad manners not to invite someone to eat if they visit when you are eating. "I think that some food left over. Come in and drink some coffee and eat something."

As Slippery Ochro quickly entered the kitchen, Dularie put her roti down, got up and washed her hands before dishing out some boulangers and roti for Slippery Ochro, while Mohabir poured some coffee, and added milk and sugar.

Slippery Ochro made himself comfortable at the table, and picked up his coffee. He told Mohabir, "After breakfast, I gon go to Suruj Bali and let him tell me which right name belong to who."

Mohabir immediately regretted his resentment at Slippery Ochro for interrupting his breakfast.

It would'a tek me the whole morning to go to Suruj Bali and get the correct names, he thought. *A little coffee and roti and fried boulanger won't make me poor.* "I glad for your help," he told Slippery Ochro. "I got some work to do at the farm. I gon work some time at the farm, and we can go to Haynes with the right names tomorrow."

Slippery Ochro smiled as he sipped his coffee. Then he threw a bombshell at Mohabir. "Yes, we gon give Haynes the right name. Since we gon be there, Haynes may want to talk to you about the evidence you gon give in Prashad case."

Mohabir spilled coffee all over his pajama top as he attempted to scratch his head with the coffee cup in his hand. Dularie recognized his agitated state, and quickly got up to take the cup from him.

"You better go and change your clothes," she said. "I gon wash your pajama today before they stain." She turned to Slippery Ochro. "Mohabir done tell you what evidence he gon give about Prashad. What Haynes got to talk with him about evidence?"

Slippery Ochro stopped eating, the wheels in his brain turning furiously as he searched for an appropriate response. "You know how lawyers stay. It not what Mohabir gon say. It's how he gon say it."

Both Mohabir and Dularie were stumped, but Dularie retorted, "What you mean, how he gon say it? He gon just open his mouth and say that Prashad been only joking."

"Haynes gon tell him what to say," Slippery Ochro countered.

Dularie was incensed. "Mohabir hear with his own ears what Prashad tell he. He don't need no lawyer to tell him what he hear."

Slippery Ochro looked at Dularie as a teacher would look at a student who had difficulties grasping a simple concept. "When I tell you that Haynes gon tell Mohabir what to say, and how to say it, I know what I talking about. You know the story about the man who chop up his wife. Looku represent him. When the police give witness that the man tell them, *Ah me wife. Me marry she. Me mind she. Me kill she.*"

Looku told the judge and jury that the man said, *Ah me wife. Me marry she. Me mind she. ME KILL SHE?* And the man get off."

Mohabir and Dularie did not know what to say, and just sat there looking at each other.

Slippery Ochro sensed their reluctance and decided to ease the pressure. "Anyway, leh we go to Haynes and give him the right names, and we gon see what he say."

Mohabir, who was silent for most of the conversation because he avoided conflict at all costs, welcomed the change of topic. "All right. You go and get the names, and leh we try and get the nine o'clock boat tomorrow, so we can go and see Haynes and come back early."

This seemed to satisfy all parties, and Slippery Ochro finished his breakfast and left.

As soon as he was out of earshot, Dularie turned to her husband. "Look how this story changing before we eye."

Mohabir said, "Leh we hear what Haynes got to say."

"Haynes gon want to win the case and gon want you to give evidence against Prashad, even if you got to lie."

Mohabir repeated his mantra. "Prashad is my friend. I gon say that he been only joking. Leh we look after the case with Dugdug and Snakeskin, and then we gon think of Prashad's case."

"You ever think that all these things happen only since Slippery Ochro and Phulmattie build their house on our land? Before now, we didn't have any quarrel with anybody. We lived a nice, peaceful life."

"I know, but we're in this situation now, and we can't do anything about it." Then he was silent for a while before he reminded his wife about what he had told her earlier, "You know that Slippery Ochro can put us out of his house, even though it is on our land?"

Dularie repeated her question. "Why you want to go in or near Slippery Ochro and Phulmattie house?"

Mohabir started scratching his head as he asked Dularie, "But how close to his house can we go? We got orange trees and the star-apple tree near his house. We can't go and pick orange or star-apple near Slippery Ochro house? If you climb the star-apple tree, you can see right in Slippery Ochro house."

Dularie was perplexed. "Why you want to look in Slippery Ochro and Phulmattie house for?" Then she thought about the situation some more. "It our fruit trees, and we got a right to pick the fruit from our fruit trees." When she noticed her husband scratching his head vigorously, she decided to placate him. "Let we handle the case with Snakeskin and Dugdug, and then we gon see what we gon do about Slippery Ochro. Come and help me wash these plates and cups and then we can rest a bit before you go to the farm." Dularie's psychology worked, as Mohabir stopped scratching his head, and went to the sink to wash his hands, before assisting Dularie to wash the dishes.

"I feel a bit tired," he told her. "Leh we go and rest. I don't feel like going to the farm today. The way I feel, if I go to weed the farm, I may cut my hand. Me head confused with right name for Dugdug and Snakeskin. Now I learn that I can't climb my own trees near Slippery Ochro house."

"You don't got to go to work if you don't want to. One thing about working for yourself, nobody can tell you anything if you don't go to work one day, or if you go late. Nobody can fire you. And we don't want a lot of money to live. We can get food from the farm, and what we sell gon give us enough money to buy groceries. And why you want to climb tree near Phulmattie house for?"

Again, Mohabir noted that Dularie emphasized Phulmattie's house, and decided to introduce a note of levity. "Now we need money to pay Haynes," Mohabir replied half-jokingly and half seriously, as they packed up the dishes and headed to bed.

It seemed as if they had just slept for a short while, when they heard a knocking on the kitchen door and Dularie, after looking at Mohabir who was coiled like a snake and snoring loudly, decided not to wake him up. When she opened the kitchen door, she was not surprised to see Slippery Ochro waving a sheet of paper.

"I got their right name,' he said triumphantly. "Snakeskin is Ram Ramlogan and Dugdug is Sugrim Bridgemohan. Where Mohabir?"

Dularie could see the disappointment on Slippery Ochro's face when she told him, "Mohabir sleeping. Leave the names with me, and I gon give him when he wake up."

"Okay. We gon catch the nine o'clock boat tomorrow and go and see Haynes. I may drop in this afternoon for a quick drink with Mohabir."

"Mohabir don't like to drink when he got business the next day," Dularie replied. When she noticed the crestfallen appearance on Slippery Ochro's face, she added, "But you and Mohabir can take a drink tomorrow when you come back from Georgetown."

Slippery Ochro's face lightened, "You right! We got to get up early tomorrow. We gon take a drink tomorrow after we see Haynes." He turned and quickly walked down the stairs, leaving Dularie holding the sheet of paper with the names.

She put the sheet of paper on the kitchen table and returned to bed, where she found Mohabir sitting on the side of the bed, holding his head between his hands. Sitting beside him, she put her arms around his shoulders. "What happened? You got a headache?"

"I had a terrible dream.".

"What you dream to give you a headache?"

"I dream that we been sleeping, and the post of our house fall down one by one, and we still inside the house. Half of the house was on the ground, and the other half was held up by two posts. And we too frighten to move. What you think the dream mean?"

Dularie kneeled in front of him. "I think that it mean that, if we not careful, things gon turn out bad. How your dream end?"

"I couldn't move, and you couldn't move. We know that we had to get out of the house, but we couldn't do anything."

"Did the house fall down?"

"No! I wake up before it fall down."

Dularie held her husband's face between her hands. "That is a good sign. The dream is a warning that we must be careful. Tomorrow, you going to see Haynes about Dugdug and Snakeskin. Don't get involved in anything else." She took a towel from the hook on the wall, and wiped the sweat off Mohabir's face. "Come eat some lunch now, and then you can rest some more if you want to."

Mohabir went to the kitchen, and headed straight to the cupboard where he kept the rum. "I need a drink before I eat, You gon take a small one with me?"

"Me heart beating fast-fast, since you tell me your dream. I gon take a drink, and see if it help."

While Mohabir retrieved the bottle from the cupboard, Dularie got two glasses and put them on the table. As Mohabir poured two tall drinks and added Pepsi, Dularie noticed that his hand was still shaking, and this discouraged her from bringing up the dream and discussing any further meaning.

After they took a few sips, it was Mohabir who raised the topic of the dream. "I gon ask Pandit Vishram what the dream mean."

"You know that I go to the mandir and that I believe in Lord Shiva and Lord Rama? But I don't believe in pandits. Most of the pandits are bandits. They only want your money and anything else you can give them. There is a lady in my village who can tell you what the dream mean. If you want, we can go and see her the day after tomorrow, after you see Haynes." Mohabir's hand was still shaking as he reached for his glass, and Dularie thought, *He so worried that he forget to scratch his head. Is that a good thing?*

"It no good if she tell we what the dream mean. We want to know what we can do about it," Mohabir observed.

"She gon tell us what to do to avoid bad luck too. She help plenty people in the village."

"All right!" Mohabir conceded, "If she can tell we how to keep away bad luck, we can go and see her. You gon eat now?"

Dularie got up to take out their lunch, which was left-overs from the previous day's meal, leaving Mohabir to finish his drink before eating. While she was dishing out their lunch, Mohabir finished his drink, and poured another one. Dularie glanced at him, but recognized that he was still shaken by his dream, and did not say anything, as she brought the two plates, and sat at the table with him. They ate in silence, each reflecting on the situation in which they found themselves, and which indeed they allowed to flourish because of their passivity.

Eventually, Dularie could bear it no longer, and suddenly blurted, "We too soft."

Although Mohabir frequently thought the same thing, he wanted clarification from his wife. "What you mean?"

"We never had any problem with Prashad or Dugdug, or Snakeskin before. Why we got problems with them now, since Slippery Ochro and Phulmattie move in? Now you got to go to court to get restraining order against young boys who run around in *shirt-tails* when you were a big man."

"We talk about that many times before."

"Yes, but we didn't do anything about it. That what I mean that we too soft."

There was a long period of silence, in which Dularie and Mohabir looked at each other, looked away and then at each other again, until Dularie mentioned the unmentionable. "What gon happen if we ask them to leave?"

"They just build their house. You mean that we should ask them to break up their house and move from our land?"

"We can tell them that we gon pay for them to build another house if they can get somebody to agree to let them build their house on their land."

"Who gon agree for Slippery Ochro and Phulmattie to build their house on their land? You think everybody stupid like we?"

Mohabir's mind was in turmoil. Naturally a peace loving, easy-going man, he found the court cases and the question of how to get Slippery Ochro out of his land extremely confusing, and he could not remember when last so many problems were swirling in his mind. In addition, the incident with Phulmattie was like a dull, steady pain which wouldn't go away.

"I tell you before, let we finish with the court case with Dugdug and Snakeskin, and Slippery Ochro case with Prashad, and then we gon see what to do," he said, as he scratched his head vigorously.

"All right, I know that we promised to stop talking about it. But they right in front of we face, and I can't help it." Then, seeing her husband so disturbed, she decided to give a positive interpretation of Mohabir's dream. "Perhaps the house post you see falling down is Slippery Ochro breaking his house and re-building it on somebody else land."

Mohabir stopped scratching his head, and was visibly relaxed. "I hope so, I see that you finished eating, also. Let we go and rest a bit. I got to get up early to go and see Haynes."

Dularie took the plates to the sink and washed her hands. "I gon wash the dishes later. Wash your hands and let we go and rest."

Chapter 11

You'll get more from being a peacemaker than a warrior
—Arnold Schwarzenegger—

Dularie and Mohabir did not like to swear, and swore only in the most exasperating of circumstances. This time it was Dularie who exclaimed, "Wha' the rass[62] that man want with us?" She was referring to Slippery Ochro, but when she opened the front door, she saw Dugdug and Snakeskin, accompanied by Heeralall and Pandit Vishram.

"Namaste," said Pandit Vishram, putting his two hands together, and bowing slightly.

There was a dramatic transformation in Dularie's behavior. "Namaste, Pandit. Namaste, Heeralall." When she turned to face Dugdug and Snakeskin, they nervously clasped their hands together.

"Namaste, Aunty," they said in unison.

Dugdug continued, "We bring Pandit and Uncle Heeralall to see Uncle Mohabir. We sorry that we get drunk and behave bad."

Dularie could not dream of sending the two men away in the presence of Pandit Vishram and Heeralall. "You all come in," she said, and the men took their shoes off by the door, walked in, and sat on the sofa.

Mohabir joined them, but decided to leave his wife to do all the talking. Snakeskin and Dugdug sat next to each other, avoiding eye contact with Mohabir, and fidgeting nervously. Mohabir did not sit opposite the two young men, choosing instead a chair at the side, so that he was not forced to look at them.

As expected, it was Pandit Vishram who broached the topic. He turned to Mohabir and told him, "Dugdug and Snakeskin come to tell you how sorry they are for insulting you. They promise that they won't do it again."

---

[62] Obscene way of asking what he wants

- 128 -

Dugdug did not wait for Mohabir to reply. "Uncle, Snakeskin and me drink too much. It wasn't we who insult you. It was the Russian Bear rum. You know how much we respect you. It won't happen again. I promise you. And nobody can touch you when me and Snakeskin around. If anybody trouble you, tell us and we gon fix them."

Mohabir was about to answer when there was a knock on the door. Dularie went to answer it and saw Slippery Ochro standing on the platform. "I see Dugdug and Snakeskin come in with Pandit and Heeralall," he announced. "I just come over to see if I can help."

Both Mohabir and Dularie thought, *He didn't come here to help. He too inquisitive, and he like to put his nose into everybody business.* However, their kind, but bordering on weak behavior caused them not to say anything. Slippery Ochro interpreted their reticence for acquiescence, and walked right into the house and sat in the last vacant chair.

He walk in as if he own this house, Mohabir thought.

Without waiting for anybody to say anything, Slippery Ochro turned to Pandit Vishram, "Pandit, I notice you come in with Heeralall, and Dugdug and Snakeskin. You know Dugdug and Snakeskin threaten to beat up Mohabir?"

Although Pandit Vishram resented Slippery Ochro's intrusion, he calmly replied, "Yes! That's why they come to make peace."

"You mean they want to beat up the man and now they want to make peace?" Slippery Ochro turned to Mohabir and told him, "I not going to sit here and let them take their eyes pass you."

Pandit Vishram, long accustomed to these outbursts, replied calmly, "They make a mistake, and they come to tell Mohabir that they sorry."

Heeralall, who has been silent so far, and had a reputation as a plain speaker, decided to give his two cents worth. Turning to Slippery Ochro, he said, "Slippery Ochro, the whole of Canal know how much you like court case. Dugdug and Snakeskin wrong to attack Mohabir, and they come to say that they sorry. What else you want them to do?"

Slippery Ochro loved an argument, and he had this one handed to him on a platter. Turning to Heeralall, he said, "Tomorrow, we gon file a restraining order against Dugdug and Snakeskin so that they can't come within five hundred yard of Mohabir. Now they come right in the man house. After the restraining order, they gon get lock up if they try something like this."

"We in Canal try to solve our own problems without getting outside people involved," Heeralall retorted. "But some people like to go to court, and spend money they don't have on lawyers." He turned to Mohabir and addressed him. "Mohabir, you part of the Panchayat which try to settle any quarrel we have in Canal. Now you gon follow Slippery Ochro and take our problem to court? Or we gon try and settle this story now?"

Mohabir said, "The Panchayat is—"

"Yes, we always let the Panchayat settle things for us in Canal," Slippery Ochro told Heeralall. "Dugdug and Snakeskin didn't know that Mohabir was part of the Panchayat when they threaten to beat him up? What respect they got for the Panchayat if they threaten to beat up a man who belong to the Panchayat? Now, when they hear that we gon drag their ass in court, they hustle to call up the Panchayat."

Heeralall's back was up. "We come to speak with Mohabir, not to you," he told Slippery Ochro.

"I representing Mohabir," Slippery Ochro shot back.

Pandit Vishram decided to intervene, and addressed Mohabir. "You are a member of the Panchayat, and you are representing Canal. Now Slippery Ochro representing you?"

Mohabir and Dularie looked at each other, each waiting for the other to say something, but both were silent. Each of them recognized that Mohabir was losing the power and respect that he previously held in Canal, but neither knew how to stop the ebb.

Mohabir told the gathering in a weak voice, "Dularie and I don't know anything about the court system, and Slippery Ochro helping us."

Slippery Ochro pounced on this opportunity. "And I gon continue to help you. Dugdug and Snakeskin want to make peace because they know that the court gon find them guilty, and they gon have a criminal record. Mohabir done nothing wrong."

Pandit Vishram attempted to pour oil on troubled waters. "Nobody said that Mohabir did anything wrong. Dugdug and Snakeskin admit that they did something wrong, and they come to apologize. That is the way we handle things in Canal."

Mohabir remembered the incidents which he and the Panchayat resolved successfully in the past, and made his decision. "If Dugdug and Snakeskin come to apologize, then I gon accept their apology, and drop the court case."

Slippery Ochro was outraged and turned to Mohabir. "You make me take you to Haynes, and he take your case. If you drop it now, you gon spoil my reputation with Haynes, and he not gon handle any more court case from me."

Heeralall replied in a firm tone, "Slippery Ochro, as I said before, you like court cases, and you trying to drag Mohabir into your court cases. If the man say that he willing to accept Dugdug and Snakeskin apology, then that is his right. Just because you live on his land, don't give you the right to rule his life?"

Slippery Ochro did not answer Heeralall, but instead turned to Mohabir and told him, "Mohabir, I grateful that you let me build my house on your land. Dugdug and Snakeskin threaten to beat you, and I take you to Haynes to get them to stop their nonsense. But if you accept their apology now, and drop your case with Haynes, me and you done."

Heeralall interjected, "You mean that you gon move your house from Mohabir's land?"

"I ain't moving me house nowhere," Slippery Ochro addressed Mohabir instead of Heeralall. "I tell you that Haynes said that *A man's house is his castle*. I gon live in my house. But if you accept the apology of these two hooligans, and spoil things between me and Haynes, me and you done."

Mohabir started scratching his head vigorously, and Dularie decided to speak for her husband. "Slippery Ochro, before you build your house on we land, we didn't know anything about lawyer and court case. Mohabir, you accept the apology from Dugdug and Snakeskin and drop the court case against them. We gon see what gon happen."

"All right." Mohabir addressed Pandit Vishram. "But tell Dugdug and Snakeskin not to behave stupid again."

Slippery Ochro got up to leave, but before he exited the door, he turned to everybody and said, "I gon go to Haynes tomorrow, and let him tell me what to do. Mohabir, you owe me money for taking you to Haynes yesterday." When he slammed the door and left, Mohabir's right hand automatically went to his head.

Everybody recognized Mohabir's discomfort, but it was Snakeskin who decided to reassure him. "Uncle Mohabir, we sorry for what happened. It won't happen again. And if anybody, including Slippery Ochro, give you trouble, we gon fix them. You don't worry about nothing."

Dugdug added, "Uncle, you and auntie always live a peaceful life. We never gon let anybody make your life difficult. People who encourage us to insult you, now encouraging you to take we to court."

"I am glad that everything work out okay," said Pandit Vishram. "Dugdug and Snakeskin, try and behave yourself, and don't drink too much. Mohabir, you know that we always try and solve our problems in Canal. I'm glad that you accept Dugdug and Snakeskin apology, and settle the matter right here."

Mohabir turned to Pandit Vishram. "Pandit, I know that you don't drink with any and everybody. But I feel so glad that we settle. I got a bottle of Russian Bear. Let me bring it out, and we gon take a drink to celebrate."

All eyes turned to Pandit Vishram hopefully, especially those of Dugdug and Snakeskin, who were feeling extremely nervous after the night's ordeal, and badly wanted a drink.

"Everybody know that I sometimes take a drink or two. What I advise against is drinking every day, or drinking until you drunk, and fight. Bring the bottle, and I gon take one drink with you."

"Two the most," Mohabir said hopefully, as he made his way to the kitchen to get the bottle of Russian Bear while Dularie, who was extremely happy that the matter was resolved without Mohabir having to go to court, got up to get the glasses.

After they left, Heeralall turned to Dugdug and Snakeskin. "You're lucky that Mohabir decided to accept your apology and didn't take you to court. If Slippery Ochro had his way, the matter would'a gone to court."

"It was Slippery Ochro who encourage us to insult him in the first place," Snakeskin told Heeralall.

"You know Slippery Ochro. He like a razor blade. He cut both sides. You should not have listened to him," Heeralall observed.

"We know better now, Uncle," Dugdug told Heeralall.

When he saw Mohabir and Dularie returning with the bottle of Russian Bear rum and glasses, Pandit Vishram decided to change the topic, and addressed Dugdug and Snakeskin. "The matter settled. Everybody in Canal respect Mohabir, and I expect the two of you to show him some respect when you meet him. Even if you meet him in the rum shop, you should tell him *Ram, Ram,* because Ram is in the rum shop too."

Pandit Vishram recognized that everybody expected him to pour the first drink, so he took the bottle of Russian Bear and poured a tall drink for himself before passing the bottle to Heeralall.

Dularie did not pour because she was the only woman present, and did not want to show disrespect to Pandit Vishram by drinking in front of him. In addition, she could not imagine herself drinking with the likes of Snakeskin and Dugdug.

When everybody finished pouring, Pandit Vishram raised his glass and made a toast. "To peace and friendship."

Everybody repeated, Dugdug and Snakeskin more loudly than the rest, "To peace and friendship," before draining their glasses.

Dularie witnessed the men feeling mellow and amicable after a drink, and she remembered that there was a bottle of rum, a quarter full, left in the cupboard, and discreetly left the company and made her way into the kitchen.

Meanwhile, the men poured a second drink with Pandit Vishram mouthing, "Last one," to himself.

Dugdug and Snakeskin kept saying how sorry they were and emphasized their commitment to protecting Mohabir repeatedly.

After he finished his second drink, Pandit Vishram got up. "I got to go now." Turning to Dugdug and Snakeskin, he continued, "Everything okay now. You all take care."

"Pandit, take one more drink before you go. We really glad that you come with us, and help settle the matter right here. Before we spend money on lawyer, we rather spend it on drinks," Dugdug said.

"It drinks what got you here," Pandit Vishram replied. "One or two is okay. But not how you all drinking." With that, he put on his shoes, and went home, leaving the others to continue drinking unfettered.

After they had drunk three quarters of the bottle, Snakeskin told Mohabir, "Uncle, let me go and buy another bottle to celebrate how everything work out."

Mohabir, feeling the effects of the drinks he had consumed, welcomed the suggestion. "If you want to buy another bottle, it okay with me, but you know that you don't have to."

"I want to, uncle. I'm sorry that—"

"If you gon buy another bottle, go and buy it," Dugdug told his friend. "You done apologize ten time already."

"All right, let we take another drink first. You gon come with me?" he asked Dugdug.

"What happen, you frighten jumbie?" Dugdug teased his friend.

"No, it dark night. Jumbie only come out on moonlight night. I just want company."

"All right. Uncle we gon dash to Prashad rum shop and we gon come back quick, quick," Dugdug told Mohabir as he and Snakeskin walked out.

When they left, Dularie came to join her husband and Heeralall. "I glad that you accept Snakeskin and Dugdug apology, so we don't got to go to court," she said to her husband. "Now Slippery Ochro angry with you. But he live on our land. What we gon do?"

Mohabir scratched his head as he turned to Heeralall, who addressed both man and wife. "You can't do anything about Slippery Ochro living on your land. You shouldn't have allowed him to build his house on your land, but that done already. The boat done gone a falls. It can't turn back. Not because he live on your land, you got to be buddy—buddy with him, and take everybody to court, because Slippery Ochro like court. Live your life like you did before Slippery Ochro build his house on your land."

"We try to," said Dularie. "But every day, either Slippery Ochro or Phulmattie come knocking at our door. Mohabir and me are peaceful people, and we don't know to tell people, *No*. Slippery Ochro and Phulmattie taking advantage of that."

"Everybody in Canal know how soft both of you are, but you can't be so soft so that people take their finger and juk you in yuh eye." Then he straightened up and asked Mohabir and Dularie, "Who own this land, you or Slippery Ochro?"

Both Mohabir and Dularie recognized the question was rhetorical and did not offer an answer. After a pause of several seconds, Heeralall continued, "You did Slippery Ochro a favor to let him build his house on your land, and you are letting him run your lives."

Mohabir and Dularie knew that this was true and did not argue, but Dularie said, "Heeralall, everything happen so quickly, that we not know what was going on, and when we realize what was happening, we not know how to stop it."

Mohabir added, "Slippery Ochro and Phulmattie so smooth that..." Then he thought of Phulmattie and himself at the farm and allowed his thoughts to linger a bit.

"You saying something," Heeralall prompted.

"Oh!" Mohabir continued. "I just thinking about something. They so smooth, that before you know it, you fall in their trap. Since they built their house on our land, they here morning, noon and night. Sometimes, Dularie and I just sit down to breakfast, and either Slippery Ochro or Phulmattie come knocking at our door for something or the other."

"That true," Dularie added. "We can't get a moment peace since they build their house on our land."

"You never tell them, *No*, and let them know that you too busy?" Heeralall asked.

"We not accustomed to turning people away from our door," Dularie replied. "And by the time we open the door, and talk to them, Slippery Ochro and Phulmattie already in the house. Now, they angry with we because we not taking Dugdug and Snakeskin to court."

"Well, at least they won't come knocking at your door any and every time," Heeralall replied.

They were interrupted by Dugdug and Snakeskin, who came in holding two bottles of Russian Bear rum. Before anybody could say anything, Dugdug addressed the group. "We buy one bottle, and we decide to open it and see if there is a picture of a Russian bear in the inside of the cork. Me and Snakeskin bet a half. I tell him that we gon see a picture of the Russian bear, and he said that we won't. I win, and we get another bottle." Then turning to Snakeskin, he said, "Now you owe me a half."

Snakeskin, still elated because Mohabir promised not to take them to court, reiterated what he earlier said, "I rather spend me money on rum than on lawyers."

The four men finished the bottle among them, while Dularie took another trip to the kitchen. It was not often that people in Canal drank with two full bottles in front of them, and Mohabir felt good about the whole evening as he looked at the bottles on the coffee table.

Their revelry was interrupted by a knock at the door, and when Heeralall, who was nearest to the door, opened it, there were Slippery Ochro and Phulmattie. When Slippery Ochro went home, he had shared with Phulmattie the evening's events, and had concluded with, "We can't make bad with Mohabir and Dularie. We living on his land, and we pick fruits, and get vegetables from his farm."

"You right," Phulmattie had replied. "I gon go with you to Mohabir and explain that you sorry for what you said. It good that he decide not to take Dugdug and Snakeskin to court. What good that gon do?"

This had been the reply that Slippery Ochro was hoping for. "Leh we go right now, while everything fresh. Put on your good dress. I gon let you talk to Mohabir and Dularie." What Slippery Ochro did not tell his wife was that he knew that Mohabir and his guests were drinking, and that he badly wanted another drink.

Slippery Ochro glanced at the two bottles of rum, while Phulmattie established eye contact with Mohabir. "Phulmattie come to talk with Mohabir," Slippery Ochro told Heeralall, and without waiting for an invitation, he and Phulmattie walked into the house.

Mohabir remembered his earlier conversation with Heeralall, and although he did not welcome Slippery Ochro's and Phulmattie's company, he was captivated by Phulmattie's look, which was bordering on being lecherous.

"Slippery Ochro come to tell you that he sorry for what he say earlier," Phulmattie told Mohabir, as she looked at him with her most seductive smile, which did not go unnoticed by Heeralall.

At this prompt, Slippery Ochro walked right up to Mohabir and stretched out his hand. Mohabir felt that he had no choice but to reach out and shake it. Slippery Ochro attempted to explain his earlier behavior. "At first, I been angry that you decide to drop the case after all the trouble we take to go to Haynes. But Phulmattie convince me that it was the right thing to settle Canal matters in Canal."

In spite of Slippery Ochro's apology, Mohabir still felt a reluctance to invite him for a drink, until Phulmattie walked right past the men to join Dularie in the kitchen.

"Heh, Dularie girl, you in the kitchen all alone. I give Slippery Ochro *good* for what he tell Mohabir. After all, you and Mohabir let we live on your land." Then she glanced at the bottle on the counter, and noticed that there was only a little rum left. "Leh we take a drink and finish the bottle. The men got two bottle, and we gon take a little from them." With that, she helped herself to a glass, and poured the remaining rum in Dularie's and her glass. They had to be satisfied with water as a chaser, because Dularie had run out of Pepsi, and was reluctant to go and take one from the coffee table with all the men around.

Meanwhile, Slippery Ochro found an empty chair, and sat down uninvited, stealing glances at Dugdug and Snakeskin, who refused to meet his eye. Mohabir had never been inhospitable any time in his life, and went to the kitchen to get a glass for Slippery Ochro.

As soon as he entered the kitchen, he was greeted by Phulmattie. "Mohabir, you mean to say that you men got two bottle rum, and you wife and she company got to go thirsty?"

Mohabir looked at Dularie, who was feeling good, but looked like she could do with another drink.

He reached for a glass, and as he made his way out of the kitchen, he addressed both women. "I gon come back in a minute."

Mohabir returned to the living room, gave Slippery Ochro his glass, and grabbed one of the full bottles. "We drinking and having a nice time," he told the men. "I gon pour a little for the ladies, and bring the rest." All the men nodded, and Mohabir noted that Slippery Ochro nodded more vigorously and longer than the rest of the men. He returned to the kitchen and poured half of the bottle in the empty bottle sitting on the table, before returning to the living room to join the others. Slippery Ochro had already poured by the time he returned, and so did the others, so Mohabir poured a drink for himself after he sat down.

Slippery Ochro raised his glass, and turning to Mohabir, he said, "I glad that things work out okay between you Dugdug and Snakeskin. We can all be friends again."

Nobody said anything in agreement or denial, and they all stifled their thoughts as they drank.

Phulmattie was doing some fence mending and politicking in the kitchen. "Gal, I glad that Mohabir did not take Dugdug and Snakeskin to court. I tell Slippery Ochro that Mohabir did the right thing. Don't worry, I gon keep Slippery Ochro in line."

Instead of replying, Dularie thought, *I know how Phulmattie and Slippery Ochro operate. I not going to say nothing. I gon just listen to her.* Phulmattie continued,

"But Dugdug and Snakeskin still wrong to insult Mohabir like they did, and now they sit down drinking together as if nothing happened," Phulmattie said.

She still trying to set strife between Mohabir and them boys, Dularie thought. "Dugdug and Snakeskin apologize, and Mohabir decide to drop the matter," she told Phulmattie in a firm voice.

Phulmattie instinctively realized that she was moving too fast. "You right. It good that they live good. I gon tell Slippery Ochro to talk with Dugdug and Snakeskin seriously and tell them not to ever let it happen again."

"They already tell Mohabir that they won't do it again." Even Dularie was surprised by her own assertiveness.

"Slippery Ochro gon make sure. Let we take another drink." Phulmattie poured drinks for Dularie and herself.

While Phulmattie was working on Dularie, Slippery Ochro was manipulating the conversation with the men. "Dugdug, Snakeskin, you lucky that Mohabir accept your apology, and not take you to court." When Dugdug and Snakeskin did not reply to him, Slippery Ochro continued, "I been want him to take you to court, you know. But he did the right thing to settle the matter right here in Canal."

Heeralall saw an opportunity and swooped on it. "Slippery Ochro, why are you taking Prashad to court? Why don't you settle things in Canal?"

The whole room was so quiet that you could clearly hear the sound of the night birds and other nocturnal creatures. Slippery Ochro squirmed, and his hand began to shake, either from anger or embarrassment, while Mohabir scratched his head vigorously.

Slippery Ochro finally replied. "I come here to tell Mohabir that I sorry that I walk out earlier, and you want to pick a quarrel with me. How the story with Prashad come in this conversation? We not talking about that now. Heeralall, if you want to pick an argument with me, fine. But not in Mohabir house. And furthermore, we not friends. If I pass you on the road, I not going to talk to you. And I don't want you to talk to me. Okay?"

The fear most of the people in Canal had for Slippery Ochro superseded Heeralall's penchant for plain speech, and he stayed quiet, although he noticed Mohabir still scratching his head vigorously. Help came from an unexpected source. Phulmattie and Dularie, after quite a few drinks, and feeling rather courageous, heard Slippery Ochro's outburst and made their way into the living room. Dularie was hardly surprised but was very concerned when she saw her husband scratching his head, and knew that she would find blood on his fingernails and marks on his scalp.

Phulmattie said. "Slippery Ochro, why you talking about Prashad. You come to apologize to Mohabir about how stupid you behave, and now I hearing about Prashad."

"Ask Heeralall why. He start it."

"If he start it, it don't mean that you have to end it. I don't want to hear another word about Prashad from you." Then she looked at Heeralall, and announced, "Slippery Ochro, if anybody want to say something about Prashad, you don't say anything. Let them knock they own drum and dance to they own music."

Dularie, who went closer to Mohabir and held his hand to prevent him scratching his head, was surprised to hear Phulmattie speaking to Slippery Ochro like she did. Phulmattie's speech gave her the courage to chastise her husband. Putting one arm around Mohabir's shoulder, she cajoled him, "Mohabir, you can't let other people get you upset. If Heeralall and Slippery Ochro want to argue about Prashad, that their business. You can't get upset about that."

"But I got to give evidence against Prashad," Mohabir answered weakly.

Dularie decided to be firm, for the sake of her husband, and to let everybody know where she and Mohabir stood on the issue. She addressed Mohabir, but the information was meant for everybody. "You gon give evidence that Prashad been joking, but only if they summons you to court. If they don't summons you, then you won't go."

Making peace was atypical of Phulmattie, but she decided that was the best strategy in the long run. "Slippery Ochro, you come to apologize to Mohabir, and you already apologize. Let we go home now." And she stood there looking at Slippery Ochro, who felt he had no choice but to get up and go home with her.

Chapter 12

Be ready for reconciliation after quarrels. You know, the purpose of reconciliation is to avoid the filibuster.

—N.K. Jemisin—

After Slippery Ochro and Phulmattie left, Heeralall told Mohabir, "Mark my advice, if you follow Slippery Ochro, you gon end up with trouble." Then he turned to Dularie, and admonished her. "I notice that you and Phulmattie very thick," as he held his index and middle fingers close together. "You know that she and Slippery Ochro work together. Don't think that you smarter than she. That lady gon buy you, and sell you, and you got to give she change."

"Since they build their house on our land, we got nothing but trouble," Dularie confessed. "But we can't do anything about it now."

Heeralall was not easily appeased. "You can let them live their own lives, and you and Mohabir live your lives."

Thus chastened, Dularie held Mohabir's hand a bit tighter, in the event that he might want to scratch his head, and Mohabir, reluctant to meet Heeralall's eyes, glared at Dugdug and Snakeskin, who squirmed uncomfortably in their seats. The evening went on in this manner until the bottles of rum were finished, and the visitors prepared to go home.

Just before he left, Heeralall delivered a last warning to Mohabir. "Everybody always respect you in Canal. You can't let a man and his wife, who only live for court cases, let you and Dularie spend your lives with lawyers and in courts." Then, without waiting for an answer, he left.

Dugdug and Snakeskin got up shortly after Heeralall's departure, and Dugdug felt an obligation to say something to Mohabir and Dularie before he left. "Uncle, Auntie, we sorry what happen. If you need anything, you just have to ask Snakeskin and me, and we gon do it." And he and Snakeskin made their way home, leaving Mohabir and Dularie to reflect on the evening's events.

"Heeralall quite right when he say that we letting Slippery Ochro and Phulmattie rule our lives," Dularie told her husband. "He is the cause people have to come to our house and tell us what to do. You used to do that for other people."

Mohabir, tired after the evening's events, put his hand on his wife's shoulder. "Heeralall right, but I tired now. Let we go to bed, and we gon talk about it in the morning."

Dularie acquiesced. "All right. You go to bed, and I'll close up and then join you." She watched her husband go off to bed, and as she went about locking the doors and closing the windows, she felt a sense of peace that she and Mohabir finally agreed—Slippery Ochro and his wife were destroying their lives! But when she thought about what they could about it, the feeling of unease returned.

Chapter 13

"True law is right reason in agreement with nature; it is of universal application, unchanging and everlasting; it is a summons to duty by its commands, and averts from wrongdoing by its prohibitions."

—Marcus Tullius Cicero—

For the next week, Mohabir and Dularie got glimpses of Slippery Ochro and Phulmattie around their hut, but there was no interaction between them, and as they enjoyed the peace and quiet, they reminded each other of how life was before Slippery Ochro and Phulmattie intruded in their lives.

They were relaxing after lunch on the Tuesday of the following week, when there was a knock on the door, and Dularie decided to answer it and let Mohabir nap.

There was a huge policeman at the door, sweat streaming his face from the exertion of riding nine miles—the distance of Mohabir's home from the Wales Police Station in the blazing sun. Even in the hot tropical climate, the Guyanese police officers had followed the tradition of the London police, and had donned the black uniform. When the policeman finished wiping the sweat off his face with a dirty white handkerchief, he reached in his shirt pocket, and pulled out a folded sheet of blue paper. As he opened the paper, Dularie could clearly read the heading *SUMMONS*.

"Good day," said the policeman, "Is Mr. Mohabir home?"

Dularie was shaking slightly, and hoped that the policeman would not notice, but she managed to say, "He resting. I gon go and get him." She left the front door open to show the policeman that she did not have anything to hide, and went to the bedroom. Mohabir was awake. "A policeman here to see you with a summons. He did not give me the summons, but ask for you."

Mohabir went to the door in his pajamas. When he saw the policeman wiping the sweat off his face, he was filled with a feeling of apprehension, knowing that his week of peace was about to come to an end.

"Mr. Mohabir?" asked the policeman.

Mohabir nodded.

"I have a summons for you to appear in court," the policeman said as he handed Mohabir the blue sheet of paper.

Mohabir accepted the summons.

The policeman said, "You have been served," and walked down the stairs, jumped on his bicycle, and cycled to Gobin's bridge to access the main road on the other side of the Canal, leaving Mohabir and Dularie to pore over the summons.

"Can you read what it says?" Dularie said. "The blue paper hurts my eyes."

Mohabir went to the landing where the light was better, and began to read. "In the matter better between Rohit Prashad and Sugrim Singh, you are hereby commanded to appear as a witness before the court on November 22, 1966." Mohabir did not read the remainder of the summons aloud. It gave the address of the Victoria Law Courts, and stated that the penalties for not appearing included a fine, imprisonment, or both. He and Dularie looked at each other for a long time, without saying anything.

"Well, we expect to get the summons," Dularie told her husband, who was using all his willpower not to scratch his head. "And you already know what evidence you gon give."

Mohabir's right hand twitched, but he made an effort and put it in his pocket, as he kept staring at the summons. His favorite color was always blue, but somehow, the blue paper did not look so appealing at that moment. Neither Mohabir nor Dularie was surprised when they saw Slippery Ochro and Phulmattie hurrying along the pathway among the coffee trees towards their house.

"We see the policeman at your house, and we know that he bring the summons for you to come to court as a witness," Slippery Ochro shouted as he neared the house. "I see Haynes last week, and he tell me that the case gon be on November 22, but he say that I don't have to tell you, and that you gon receive a summons. I was going to tell you later today, but I see the policeman, and I know that he come to give you the summons."

Mohabir looked at Dularie. Everybody was silent for a long time, until the silence was broken by Phulmattie. "Prashad gon get what coming to him," she announced.

When Mohabir started to scratch his head, Dularie's concern for her husband made her courageous and she quickly informed Phulmattie, "Mohabir gon tell the truth, that Prashad been only joking."

Phulmattie retorted, "Wait until Haynes get him on the witness stand. He read Prashad mind that he only joking?"

Dularie asked Phulmattie, "Haynes can change the truth?"

Phulmattie remembered when she was in court one time and a lawyer was cross examining a witness who swore that he was telling the truth. "Whose truth?" the lawyer asked the witness. She decided to use the same words with Dularie.

"Whose truth?" she asked Dularie, as Mohabir scratched his head more vigorously.

"November twenty-second is next week Friday," Slippery Ochro decided to change the topic, and told Mohabir, "We got to get the seven-thirty ferry. We can go in the same car."

Dularie moved closer to her husband, put her arms around him, between his waist and shoulders, thus pinning his arms to his sides, and answered Slippery Ochro. "When you get dressed, you can get a car, and when Mohabir is dressed, he gon get a car."

Slippery Ochro twisted his mouth in displeasure, as he looked at Phulmattie for some hint as to how he should reply. Phulmattie's face, however, remained impassive.

"I got to go to the farm. Grass take over my cassava plants," Mohabir told Slippery Ochro."

"You want me to come and help you?" Phulmattie asked, revealing her gold teeth.

Mohabir remembered the last time Phulmattie went to help him in the farm, and did not want a repeat of what happened, especially in light of the present situation, but did not know how to respond,

Dularie came to his rescue. "I gon go and help him," she told Phulmattie. Then she turned to Mohabir. "We got food left over from last night. We can have it for lunch. I like going to the farm with you sometimes."

Phulmattie's face contorted with disappointment, frustration, and anger, but Mohabir was pleased by Dularie's promise to accompany him to the farm. She did not often go with him to work in the coffee and vegetable farms, but he considered it a treat whenever she did.

"I gon go and sharpen the cutlasses," he told Dularie. "You pack something for lunch and get the water ready." He left to get the cutlasses from the kitchen, leaving Slippery Ochro and Phulmattie no alternative, but to go home.

**

"You notice how they change?" Slippery Ochro asked his wife as they dejectedly walked along the path among the coffee trees to their home.

"Mohabir don't want to give evidence against Prashad," Phulmattie answered. "But he got to tell the truth when he go on the witness stand."

"Leh we not go back to their house until after the trial," Slippery Ochro responded. "We talk enough about the case, and I don't want to quarrel with Mohabir before the case."

'You're right. Leh we keep to ourselves until after the case."

**

Mohabir and Dularie got to enjoy a bit of privacy until November 22 loomed, and Mohabir had to prepare for his big court date. On the day before, he and Dularie took out his best shirt and trousers, and ironed them using an iron heated with hot coals, while Mohabir polished his black shoes to a shine. When he was finished, he found the clothes brush and carefully brushed his Wilson hat.

The following morning, Mohabir and Dularie got up early. Dularie put on the water to boil for coffee, and prepared the breakfast of roti and fried bora,

Mohabir shaved and showered. Then he put on some aftershave, which had been sitting on the dresser for longer than he could remember. The bottle was only about a quarter full, the remainder having evaporated. He looked for the bottle of cologne which he had bought on an impulse some years before when he had visited Bookers Stores in Georgetown, but could not find it.

"Dularie, where is me bottle of cologne?"

"I threw it away. You weren't using it, and it was just taking up space in the dresser."

"Well, can I use some of your perfume?"

"You want to smell like a woman? People gon laugh at you."

"All right. I don't need cologne. I sweet already." And he laughed seductively.

"Yes, you sweet and nice. Come and put on your trousers and shirt now. I iron them for you. And don't go sweet-talking the ladies now. Remember who iron your clothes, so that you can look nice."

And the bantering continued until Mohabir was ready to go by the roadside to wait for a hire car. Only then did he realize that Dularie was bantering with him, because both were nervous, and she was attempting to make him feel at ease. After about fifteen minutes, he saw Sedan's car approaching, and he flagged it. Imagine his surprise when he saw Prashad sitting in the front seat! He immediately felt anxious, but nevertheless grateful that he was sitting in the back seat. Prashad did not look back, although he saw Mohabir enter the car. Another passenger was sitting on the front seat near Prashad, and two others were in the back seat. Although the entire Canal knew about the court case between Prashad and Slippery Ochro, and of Mohabir's involvement in the case, nobody said anything, and the silence became so uncomfortable that Mohabir felt that he had to break it.

"Prashad, you know that I got to go as a witness. A policeman bring a summons to me. But I gon tell the truth that you been only joking. I gon say that you and me always joking with each other." When Prashad did not answer, and continued looking straight ahead, Mohabir felt very uncomfortable, as did everybody in the car.

Sedan felt an obligation to make his passengers comfortable. "You and Prashad been friends for a long time," he told Mohabir. "Don't make this court case come between you."

"They summons me, so I got to go," Mohabir told Sedan, although the information was meant for everybody in the car. "But I gon tell the truth. Prashad and me have been friends since we were small, and he been only joking"

When Prashad still did not answer, Buddy Boy, another passenger in the car decided to fill the gap. "I know that you will not lie and put Prashad in trouble, but them lawyers have a way of twisting your words. Remember when Chunilall chop Baba hand and the case went to court. The police charge Chunilall with chopping off Baba hand, and Chunilall hired Looku. When Looku questioned Baldeo, who took Baba to the hospital, Baldeo said that Baba hand was just hanging by the skin, and he had to cut off the skin to take Baba to the doctor. Looku argued that the police charged Chunilall with chopping off Baba hand. If Baldeo had to cut the skin off the hand, then Chunilall did not cut off the hand. And Chunilall got off."

Mohabir addressed Buddy Boy directly. "I gon say that Prashad been only joking. How they gon twist that?"

"Mohabir, you too nice, and you believe that everybody nice too. You got people in this world who gon take advantage of yuh niceness. I only hope that Haynes don't wrap you around like a camoudie, and then swallow you."

Then Buddy Boy turned to Prashad. "Prashad, you hire any lawyer?"

Prashad spoke for the first time. "I work hard and run me business. I charge everybody a fair price. I don't adjust my scales, and anybody who buy a pound of sugar from me can be sure that they get sixteen ounce, sometimes more. I get along nice with everybody. Now, I got to pay a lawyer because I make a joke with somebody I know since we been small."

Mohabir seized the opportunity to clarify his position. "Prashad, I didn't tell Slippery Ochro anything, you know. Phulmattie went home and tell him what you say. And I say right away that you been only joking."

"How come you and Slippery Ochro become so close? Me and you been friends since we been small, and we used to walk to school together."

Buddy Boy answered for Mohabir. "Slippery Ochro and Phulmattie sweet talk Mohabir and Dularie, and get them to agree for them to allow them to build a house on their land. Then they force themselves on them as friends. Many people choose their friends, but Mohabir and Dularie did not choose Slippery Ochro and Phulmattie as their friends. Slippery Ochro and Phulmattie choose Mohabir and Dularie as their friends. How can Mohabir and Dularie refuse to be friends with them when they live on their land?"

Prashad was still not appeased, and asked Mohabir directly, "If they ask you to live in yuh house, you gon let them? Now they want to take away me house and land."

"Nobody gon take away your house and land. I tell you many time that I gon speak the truth that you been only joking."

Prashad did not reply, and the silence lasted until Sedan parked the car at Vreedenhoop, and the passengers disembarked and hurried to line up to purchase their tickets for the ferry. Prashad and Mohabir found themselves on opposite ends of the ferry, which was packed.

Buddy Boy cautioned Mohabir. "You got to be careful not to let the lawyers trip you up."

Mohabir thought about the simple life he and Dularie wanted to live and tried to figure how he got involved with courts and lawyers. He also thought of how close he and Prashad were, and prayed to Lord Shiva that they would be close again, when everything was finished.

When they disembarked at the Stabroek Stelling, Prashad deliberately stayed back, while Mohabir walked ahead, crossed Water Street and then Lombard Street before entering the grounds of the Victoria Law Courts, with an imposing statute of Queen Victoria on the western side of the building. Palms on the edge of the property waved gracefully in the light breeze. The green of the trees was in sharp contrast to the red paint on the building, which almost filled the entire block.

The Victoria Law Courts did not have an area for people who waited for their cases to be heard. Instead, these people waited on the covered verandah, which ran along the east side of the building.

Mohabir went up the stairs, and was met by Haynes, dressed in an immaculate black suit, and Slippery Ochro, who was dressed in black trousers and a white and blue striped shirt. Both shirt and trousers were obviously washed, but not ironed. Mohabir thought of Dularie ironing his shirt and trousers, and wondered why Phulmattie did not iron Slippery Ochro's clothes. What he did not know was that Haynes instructed Slippery Ochro to dress that way, to present an image of a poor person being maligned by a rich storekeeper.

Mohabir did not meet Slippery Ochro's eyes, and chose to look at Haynes who greeted him. "Welcome, Mr. Mohabir. I am so glad that you can come and give evidence on behalf of Sugrim Singh. The judge will call up the case, and ask Prashad whether he pleads guilty or not guilty. He will plead not guilty, and the judge will most likely postpone the case until another date."

Mohabir thought of his nice house and his farm, and the leisurely pace at which he lived his retirement days, and resented having to get up early in the morning, dress in his best clothes, and get a hire car to get the 7:30 ferry, only to be told that the case will be postponed. He asked Haynes in as angry a voice as he could muster "So I didn't need to come today?"

Haynes was unperturbed. "We need to show the judge and Prashad's lawyer that we have a witness who can prove that he maligned Slippery Ochro and his wife. And I need to talk to you further about your testimony."

Haynes was so confident, and Mohabir was so awed by the surroundings that he maintained, a sullen silence. When he glanced at the other end of the verandah and saw Prashad conversing with Looku, he knew right away that Prashad had—he thought of the big word that Haynes had used, but could not remember it—and settled for *hired* Looku.

Haynes and Slippery Ochro followed his glance and saw Prashad and Looku. "I see that Prashad has retained Looku," Haynes observed.

Oh! That's the word, Mohabir said to himself. Why do lawyers like to use fancy words? Why did he not simply use *hire*? And we have to pay them to use these fancy words. Then he looked in the Prashad's direction, and thought, *He gon win this case if he hire Looku.*

They continued talking until the court attendant announced, "Mr. Rohit Prashad and Mr. Sugrim Singh."

As Mohabir accompanied Haynes and Slippery Ochro, he glanced in Prashad's direction, and saw that he and Looku were making their way to the entrance of the courtroom. Haynes led the party to the section to their left, while Looku and Prashad sat in the section on the right. Except for the time when he had bought the house and land in which he was living, and had to have the *Transport* for the house and land to be transferred to his name, it was the first time that Mohabir was in a courtroom. He was awed by the situation, and especially by the elevated judge's desk. It reminded him of the primary school, where there were open classrooms, and the headmaster's desk was on a raised platform. All the students, and most of the teachers, were afraid of the headmaster, who often humiliated the junior teachers and some of the senior teachers, in front of the entire school.

The low murmur of conversation stopped when the bailiff announced, "All rise! Court is now in session. Justice Dan Jappan presiding."

Everybody stood, most with their eyes fixed on the door from where the judge was supposed to walk through. About five seconds later, a portly gentleman, with an impassive face, and wearing a white wig and black gown, entered the courtroom. As he stood behind the imposing desk, he nodded to all present and said formally, "Please be seated." Then he took some time to read the docket in front of him, and announced, "In the matter between Rohit Prashad and Sugrim Singh, Sugrim Singh is claiming damages to the extent of ten thousand dollars, because Prashad slandered his wife."

He directed his gaze to Prashad. "Mr. Prashad, are you represented by counsel?"

Looku stood up and answered for Prashad. "If it please Your Honor, Mr. Prashad has retained me as his counsel."

"Is your client going to contest the case, Mr. Looku?"

"Yes, Your Honor. And we request a trial by jury, Your Honor."

"Mr. Singh, I see that you are accompanied by Mr. Haynes. Is he your counsel?"

Haynes promptly stood up and addressed the judge. "I have the privilege of representing Mr. Sugrim Singh, Your Honor. And the defendant's request for a trial by jury is okay with us."

"All right. I am glad that we got that out of the way. The trial is set for...," Justice Dan Jappan paused while he examined the calendar on his desk, "December tenth. We will convene a jury then to hear the merits of your arguments and make a decision." Then the judge banged his gavel, and rose to enter his chambers.

As he walked out of the courtroom with Haynes and Slippery Ochro, Mohabir felt a sense of relief that he did not have to give evidence,. After a few minutes, though, he thought, *I give up working in the farm, and take all the trouble to come here, and the whole thing take five minutes. That why I never liked to do anything with the police and courts. I really sorry that I got involved with Slippery Ochro and all his court business.*

When they were on the verandah, Haynes placed his hand on Mohabir's shoulder and told him, "I already talked with Sugrim Singh about what he should say when I call him as a witness. I would like you to come to my office for a few minutes so that I can talk with you about the evidence you are going to give."

Already angry that he basically gave up the entire day to spend five minutes in the courtroom, Mohabir replied, "I can tell you right now what evidence I gon give. I gon say that Prashad ask me if I take a second wife when he saw me with Slippery Ochro wife, but he been only joking."

"It's not as simple as that," Haynes said.

Mohabir was confused. "What do you mean?"

Haynes adopted a tone as if he were speaking to a child. "You say Prashad was joking. How do you know that he was joking?" Then, as his own arguments formulated in his mind, he continued, "You know what, you don't have to come to the office. Just say what you just told me."

**

In the ferry across the river, Mohabir saw Prashad sitting on a bench near the entrance facing them. Prashad scowled and turned away, so they found a seat at the opposite end. Things were far from comfortable between Slippery Ochro and Mohabir, because Mohabir blamed Slippery Ochro for spoiling things between him and his long-time friend.

Slippery Ochro sensed that Mohabir was not inclined to talk with him, and stayed with him for the sake of appearances, but did not initiate any conversation, except to say to Mohabir, "Haynes know what he doing. I wonder what argument Looku planning." When Mohabir maintained a stubborn silence, Slippery Ochro did not say anything until they disembarked at Vreedenhoop.

"Prashad always take Polo car. Let we go with Budya car," he told Mohabir.

Mohabir struggled for something to say, but came up empty, and mutely accompanied Slippery Ochro to Budya's car, as Prashad, predictably, went to Polo's car.

Budya was still hustling passengers as they entered the car, but as soon as he got six passengers, and he sat behind the wheel, he asked Slippery Ochro, "So what did the judge say about your case?"

"You know how these court things slow?" Slippery Ochro answered. "Today, the judge just ask Prashad if he going to contest the case or not. Prashad must have a lot of money, because he hired Looku. And Looku tell the judge that they gon fight the case. And the judge set the case for December tenth."

Mohabir thought that it was the right time to vent. "I got up early. I shave, bathe, and put on my best clothes to spend five minutes in the kiss-me-ass courtroom, only to hear that the judge set another date to hear the case."

"That how the court system work," Slippery Ochro explained to Mohabir. "The judge didn't know whether Prashad will contest the case or not. This not a criminal case, so they don't have to have a jury. Many people ask for the judge alone to decide. The judge can't waste time getting a jury until he know what the people agree to. Sometime, the person filing the complaint want one thing, and the person that he is filing the complaint against want something else. Then the judge got to decide. The judge got to be very careful, because if there is an appeal, and the appeal court find that the judge make an error, that will be held against him. Imagine if every case brought before a judge, there is an appeal, and the appeal court find that the judge make an error, then the government might decide that he not fit to be a judge."

Budya, feeling that he had learnt enough, said, "So the case postpone. And Prashad hired Looku. That gon be an interesting case." Then, without giving Slippery Ochro an opportunity to continue his expostulation, he asked another passenger in his car, "Babulall, you finish picking your coffee yet?"

All the passengers felt relieved. As much as they recognized Slippery Ochro's expertise in the legal arena, they felt that they had learnt enough.

"I almost finish," Babulall replied. "Laborers hard to get now, because everybody picking coffee. I only manage to get two people to help me pick, and I had to pay them extra."

"I hear that coffee price gone down," Budya remarked. "Plenty people cut down their coffee tree, and plant sugar cane. Wales estate buying the sugar cane from them. They say that it pay better than coffee."

"That good for people who already got money," Babulall said. "To plant cane, you got to pay people to cut down your coffee tree. Then you got to plough your land. Then plant cane. You got to spray the cane. Then pay cane cutters, who charge more than I pay the women to pick coffee. Then you sell it to Wales Estate. How I gon mind my family while I do all those thing? I already got coffee trees, and I get a little money every year. I gon make do with that."

Budya conceded. "You're right! Look at all the people who cut down their coffee trees and plant cane. Jainandan Singh is a teacher, and he get a salary. Matthew rich, and he got a big farm. He cut down only half of his coffee tree, and he plant cane. He still getting money from half of his coffee tree."

Slippery Ochro did not appreciate being sidelined. "Samlall take Jainandan Singh to court because Jainandan Singh spray his cane, and some of the spray went in his farm where he plant cassava and plantain. Most of his plantain and cassava plants dead, and Jainandan Singh had to compensate Samlall. Samlall drink and boast at Manbahal rum shop that he get more money from Jainandan Singh than he would'a get if he would'a sell the cassava and plantain."

Budya was not to be dissuaded from changing the topic. "That past and gone," he told Slippery Ochro. "Now Jainandan Singh and Samlall are good friends. Mohabir, you want to drop in at Manbahal and try a quick quarter? I would'a invite you to go to Prashad, but I notice that your spirit gone from Prashad."

"Prashad spirit gone from me," Mohabir replied. "I tell him that I got a summons and I got to go to court to give evidence, but I gon tell the truth. But Prashad still vex with me."

"He gon come round," Budya said. "Let me drop the passenger off and then we gon come back and take a quick drink."

When they reached Gobin's bridge, Budya automatically stopped so that Slippery Ochro could get out. When Slippery Ochro didn't budge, Budya asked him, "You want to stop here?"

"I thought that we going to Manbahal for a drink?" Slippery replied.

Budya and Mohabir were stumped. Neither wanted Slippery Ochro to join them for a drink, but both were too nice, or not strong enough to bluntly refuse him.

Budya weakly said, "You want to come, too?" and drove off.

When he dropped all the passengers off, and he, Mohabir and Slippery Ochro went into Manbahal's rum shop, Budya intended to buy a quarter bottle of rum for himself and Mohabir, but when Slippery Ochro joined the company, he knew that a quarter bottle would not be enough, and he asked for a half bottle at the counter. Budya knew that Slippery Ochro's presence would prevent him from discussing what he wanted to talk with Mohabir about, and decided that he would just have a quiet drink with Mohabir, notwithstanding Slippery Ochro's presence.

That was not to be. As soon as he sat down after putting the bottle of rum and the glasses on the table, and everybody poured drinks and chasers, Slippery Ochro raised his glass and said, "We got Prashad where we want him now. Mohabir always said that he gon say that Prashad was joking. Haynes said that he can say so on the witness stand. Haynes gon deal with it."

"Slippery Ochro, I just want to take a quiet, lil drink with Mohabir," Budya told him. Then gathering some courage, he added, "I didn't invite you, but you want to come, and I didn't stop you."

Slippery Ochro took the hint and stayed silent, busying himself by pouring himself his drinks and chasers.

Budya turned to Mohabir. "I know the situation in which you find yourself. Everybody in Canal respect you. Now you find yourself mix up with a court case, and you and Prashad don't talk. I don't know what advice to give you, except to speak the truth, and hope for the best. I gon take a drink with you, and pray that everything work out for you." He and Mohabir raised their glasses, and were surprised when Slippery Ochro raised his glass with them. Budya and Mohabir were ill at ease for the remainder of the time they spent together, but Slippery Ochro seemed quite comfortable, although he said little. When the bottle was finished,

Budya left to make another trip to Vreedenhoop, and Mohabir felt that he had little choice, but to walk home with Slippery Ochro.

Neither said anything until they reached Gobin Bridge which they had to take to cross the canal to access their homes.

"I know you don't like court, and I sorry that I bring you into this," Slippery Ochro told Mohabir. "I gon give you some of the money I gon get from Prashad, when I win the case."

Mohabir, who was already incensed because he had wasted the entire day on a court case that was postponed, stopped walking and turned to Slippery Ochro, "You think I want Prashad money, or your money? I not a parasite." Mohabir was about to say, *Like you*, but stopped himself just in time. Instead, he said, "I only eat my own sweat. I don't want anybody money. My wife and I eat only what we get from our land, or what we can buy with our own money, so don't tell me any nonsense about giving me some of the money you gon get from Prashad."

Slippery Ochro had never seen Mohabir angry like this, and never expected him to speak so forcefully. "I sorry that you waste the whole day on the court case. If you have any work to do in the farm, Phulmattie and I gon help you for a day or two. You don't have to pay us."

Mohabir remembered the time when Phulmattie went to help him, and the guilt he had to deal with afterwards. "Dularie gon come with me to the farm," he told Slippery Ochro as they approached their homes.

**

Slippery Ochro and Phulmattie stayed away from Mohabir and Dularie for the next few days, sensing that the couple was angry with them. When Mohabir was served the second summons to attend court as a witness, he and Dularie were not as awed as when they were served the first, but they still resented the fact that Slippery Ochro and Phulmattie were the reason that they had to break their comfortable routine and spend time in the courts in Georgetown.

When the policeman left, Mohabir took the summons to the kitchen, and Dularie sat opposite him. "*You are commanded to appear before the court on December 10...*" it began.

"They are commanding me," Mohabir told Dularie. "In my life, nobody ever command me, and now two time, they commanding me."

Dularie got up and sat near her husband. "You go to court on December tenth, and give your evidence. And then we finish with court case," she told him soothingly.

"As long as Slippery Ochro and Phulmattie living on our land, we gon never finish with court case."

Dularie was silent, knowing that Mohabir was correct, and prayed that something would happen to encourage Slippery Ochro and Phulmattie to leave their land.

Chapter 14

"Thus went my first Court Day. I think I'm going to puke."

—Tamora Pierce, *Terrier*—

On December 10, Mohabir and Slippery Ochro went to Georgetown in separate cars. They hadn't spoken to each other for quite some time, although they had glimpses of each other between the trees on Mohabir's property. When they reached the Victoria Law Courts, they went on opposite ends of the verandah, until Haynes signaled Mohabir to join him along with Slippery Ochro.

Haynes told Mohabir, "So you will give evidence that Prashad told you that it looked as if you took a second wife, but that he was only joking?"

"Yes, Prashad and me always joking."

"Okay. You can say that," Haynes replied.

When the court orderly called out, "Sugrim Singh and Rohit Prashad," everybody connected with the case filed into the courtroom, with Prashad and Looku sitting on the opposite section from Haynes, Slippery Ochro, and Mohabir. After a few minutes, the court orderly announced, "All rise! Court is now in session. Justice Dan Jappan presiding."

"Please be seated," Justice Dan Jappan said as he sat down with a flourish and reached for the docket.

After about thirty seconds, Justice Dan Jappan looked at Prashad, and read the plaintiff's complaint, "Mr. Prashad, Mr. Sugrim Singh is claiming that you maligned and slandered his wife, in that you indicated that Mr. Mohabir took his wife, Phulmattie, as his second wife. Do you contest this claim?"

Looku stood up, along with Prashad. Looku was dressed in an immaculate black suit, his thick grey hair parted neatly in the middle, and the hair combed to the sides. Many people who had encountered Looku had imitated this style, and parted their hair in the middle, instead of on the side. "If it pleases Your Honor, Mr. Prashad has retained me to represent him, and my client intends to contest this claim."

Justice Dan Jappan glanced at Looku with a surprised look. It was not often that one of the Lookus would slip up in court, and the judge was feeling amused that one of them made an error in his court. "Does your client INTEND to contest the claim, or does he contest it?"

"I apologize, Your Honor. My client contests this claim."

"All right! Mr. Haynes, can you call your first witness?"

Mr. Haynes, dressed in a dark striped suit, and a blue tie, with his hair slicked back, stood up confidently and, with his British accent, announced, "The plaintiff would like to call Phulmattie Singh to the witness stand."

He turned and nodded to Phulmattie, who wore a long white dress and a white orhni. If she intended to look chaste, she succeeded to the superficial observer. A more acute person, however, would have been able to see the cunning and harshness etched on her face, as she walked demurely to the witness stand, where she was sworn in by the court official.

Haynes asked Phulmattie, "Did you accompany Mr. Mohabir to Mr. Prashad's shop on the night of January 14, 1966?"

Phulmattie, who looked quite comfortable in the witness stand, answered, "Yes, sir."

"And when you entered Prashad's shop. What did Prashad say to Mohabir?"

Phulmattie always found tears a useful weapon and decided to make use of her arsenal. Tears flowed freely as she replied, "He look at me from head to toe, and tell Mohabir that it looked as if he take a second wife." Then she pulled her handkerchief out of her pocket and sobbed uncontrollably. Between sobs, she announced, "Since I marry Slippery Ochro, another man never hold me hand. And then Prashad tell Mohabir something like that." Then she continued sobbing so much that she could not speak.

Haynes turned to the judge. "Your Honor, the witness is understandably upset. I request a brief recess, in order that she can compose herself."

"I am ordering a recess of fifteen minutes. Mr. Haynes, please calm your witness down, so we can continue with the case."

"Thank you for understanding, Your Honor," Haynes told the judge as he stretched his hand out to help Phulmattie out of the witness stand.

Phulmattie reached out to take Haynes's hand but remembered just in time her statement about another man not holding her hand since she got married, and she came down from the witness stand unassisted, but still sobbing.

Slippery Ochro met her as she stepped out of the witness stand, took her hand, and led her to her seat in the second row. He took out his handkerchief which she used to blow her nose, while Slippery Ochro was telling her, loud enough for the onlookers to hear, "I know how it hurt you to have Prashad telling you what he did, but you got to stop crying, and tell the judge and jury what happened."

With great effort, Phulmattie eased up on her sobbing, emitting only the occasional groan, and when the court orderly announced, "All rise! Court is now re-convened," she was relatively quiet. The only evidence of her crying was the handkerchief she used to dab her eyes.

"Mr. Haynes, is your client ready to proceed?"

"Yes, Your Honor. She was overwrought by the emotions which the memory of the incident produced, but she is quite calm now."

"Okay. You may resume the questioning of the witness."

Phulmattie, with Slippery Ochro's handkerchief in her left hand, returned to the witness stand, and Haynes approached her.

"Mrs. Singh, let me remind you that you are still under oath. You stated earlier that when Prashad saw you with Mohabir, he told Mohabir that it look as if he take a second wife."

"Yes, I don't know why he said that. It is because we poor, and we ask Mohabir if we could build a small house on his land." Phulmattie started sobbing again.

"Take a deep breath, Mrs. Singh. I would not like to ask the judge for another adjournment." Haynes looked at the judge, and smiled, as Justice Dan Jappan nodded. "And how did that make you feel?"

Phulmattie started crying again, and the court was silent for a few minutes until she was able to speak.

"It make me feel small and worthless," she told Haynes. "Just because we poor..." And she started sobbing,

Haynes looked at the jury, which included five women, and noticed that two of them also pulled out their handkerchiefs. "I have no more questions for the witness," he told the judge as he returned to his seat.

"Mr. Looku, do you have any questions for the witness?" Justice Dan Jappan said.

"Just a few questions, Your Honor." Looku walked confidently towards the witness stand. Approaching Phulmattie, he asked her, "I see that you were quite upset when you remembered that Prashad told Mohabir that it looked as if he had taken a second wife."

Phulmattie was taken aback. *Whose side is he on?* she asked herself. "Yes, he had no right to say that, just because we poor." She thought about crying again, but decided against it. *He trying to smart me out. I will not let that happen. He may be a big shot lawyer, but I, too, see some court cases.*

"I am glad that you are so concerned about your reputation," Looku said, "Canal is a small village, and people talk about each other a lot. Don't they?"

"Oh yes! The people in Canal like they don't have anything to do, and they walk with their mouth. If you fart, they talk about it." The entire courtroom started to laugh and Phulmattie felt proud that she could say something that could make the courtroom laugh. "That's why when Prashad tell Mohabir that it look as if he take a second wife, I know that the whole Canal gon wonder if it true. A man never hold me hand since I marry Slippery Ochro." Then she started sobbing again, but not to the extent that it would disrupt the proceedings.

"Were there any customers in the shop when you and Mohabir went?"

"No, it was a dark night and people go to sleep early."

"Why did you and Mohabir go to Prashad at eight pm on a dark night?"

Phulmattie hesitated for a few moments, wondering what Looku was trying to do. She thought about lying, but when she glanced at the seats, she saw Prashad, and knew that she had to tell the truth. "We go to buy a bottle of rum," she said.

"You went to buy a bottle of rum with Mohabir at eight o'clock on a dark night? Why did you accompany Mohabir? Was he afraid?"

Phulmattie looked at Haynes for help. When she saw that no help was forthcoming from that quarter, she looked at Slippery Ochro, who couldn't help her either. Then she had an idea. "Mohabir, his wife, Dularie, Slippery Ochro and me were taking a few drinks, and the rum finish. When Mohabir get up to buy another bottle, I notice that he staggering. I didn't want him to go and buy the rum by himself, because I was afraid that he might fall down."

"And what would you have done, had he fallen down, or if he was about to fall down?"

"I would'a hold him to steady him."

"You would have held his hand to prevent him falling?"

"Yes, I..." Phulmattie realized her mistake and was silent until Looku prompted her.

"Mrs. Singh, you were going to say that you would have held his hand to prevent him from falling down?"

Phulmattie decided to take the plunge. "Yes, I would have held his hand to stop him from falling."

"So, for the first time since you married Mr. Singh, you were prepared to hold a man's hand. A man you were accompanying to buy a bottle of rum, because the bottle of rum you were drinking with him and the others was finished?" Looku glanced at the jury, and noticed that the women who were holding handkerchiefs no longer had them. Instead, they were looking at Phulmattie with rather stern faces.

Again, Phulmattie looked at Haynes, and then at Slippery Ochro. Again, she received no help from them. The only way Phulmattie figured that she could buy more time to think was to start crying. And she did. Looku was silent for a while until Phulmattie felt that she had bought enough time.

"Yes, because they so kind that they allow me and my husband to build a small house on their land. Or else, we gon have to sleep on the street."

Looku continued his cross examination. "You said that Canal is a small village, and people like to talk."

"Yes! They mouth run like river water."

"And you didn't think that people would talk about you and Mr. Mohabir going to buy a bottle of rum in the night?"

Phulmattie was stumped. After portraying herself as a chaste woman, how was she going to justify going with Mohabir alone to buy rum in the night. "I afraid that Mohabir gon fall down and hurt himself," she replied weakly.

"Was anybody else concerned about Mr. Mohabir falling down because he had too much to drink?"

"All of we concerned."

"Then why didn't Mr. Singh go with him?"

Phulmattie stayed silent, and again looked at Haynes for rescue.

Out of pity for her, Haynes got up. "Objection, Your Honor! Mrs. Singh cannot answer for the state of mind of her husband."

Justice Dan Jappan looked at Phulmattie with something like pity. "Objection sustained. Mr. Looku, I suppose that you will have a chance to cross examine Mr. Singh later. You can ask him your questions about his reason for not accompanying Mr. Mohabir then."

"I'm sorry, Your Honor. I have no more questions for this witness," Looku told the judge as he returned to his seat.

Justice Dan Jappan said, "Mr. Haynes, please call your next witness."

"Thank you, Your Honor. I'd like to call Mr. Mohabir to the stand."

Mohabir wanted to scratch his head, but placed his hands in his pocket as he walked nervously to the witness stand. As the court orderly gave him a bible to swear on, he wanted to object, but did not feel confident enough to do so. Besides, his head was itching terribly, and he was expending all his energy in trying not to scratch it. He mechanically put his hand on the bible and swore to "tell the truth, the whole truth, and nothing but the truth."

"Mr. Mohabir, did you and Mrs. Phulmattie go to buy a bottle of rum at Prashad on the evening of January 14, 1966?"

Mohabir scratched his head vigorously as he answered, "Yes."

"And when he saw you with Mrs. Singh, did Prashad tell you that it looked as if you've taken a second wife?"

"Yes, but he was just—"

"Just *Yes* or *No* would suffice." Mohabir was not sure what "suffice" meant, but stayed silent. "And what did you say when Prashad told you that it looked as you've taken a second wife?"

"I didn't say anything, because I knew that he was joking."

"Are you a mind reader? How do you know that he was joking?"

"Prashad and I always joke with each other, and tease each other."

"Did you ever tease Prashad about somebody else's wife?"

"No, because I never see him with somebody else wife." Mohabir felt that he said the wrong thing as soon as he said it. Haynes paused and looked at the jury before he asked the next question.

"And you did not say anything to object when Prashad told you that it looked as if you've taken a second wife?"

"No."

"If you thought that Prashad was joking, did you smile? It is customary to laugh or at least smile at a joke."

"I smiled, because I knew that he was joking."

"Or because you liked the thought of having Mrs. Singh, somebody else's wife, as your second wife? Which one is it?"

"I smile because of his joke. I satisfy with one wife."

" I have no more questions for this witness, Your Honor."

Haynes strode to his seat, and Looku got up even before the judge told him, "Your witness, Mr. Looku."

"Thank you, Your Honor. Mr. Mohabir, did you think it strange that another man's wife accompanied you to buy a bottle of rum at eight o'clock on a dark night?"

Mohabir started to scratch his head as he thought of an answer. "Well, we been drinking, and the rum finish. Phulmattie accompany me to buy another bottle."

"You didn't answer the question, Mr. Mohabir. Let me rephrase. In a small village like Canal, where people gossip a lot, did you not think it strange that Mrs. Singh accompanied you to buy a bottle of rum at eight o'clock on a dark night?"

Knowing that all eyes were on him, Mohabir exerted all his will power and stopped scratching his head. "I didn't think of it at that time. It was dark, and Phulmattie didn't want me to fall down and hurt myself."

"Did you ask her to accompany you to the rum shop to buy more rum?"

"No. She offer to come with me."

"Just so that everybody can understand clearly. You, your wife, Mr. Singh and Mrs. Singh were drinking rum under your house. The rum finished, and only Mrs. Singh offered to go with you to go to the rum shop to buy another bottle. Is that correct?"

"Yes."

Looku changed his line of questioning. "You and Mr. Prashad were always joking with each other, right?"

Mohabir began to feel more relaxed after Looku asked this question. "Yes, Prashad and me always teasing each other."

"Did you take him seriously when he told you that it look as if you take a second wife?"

"No, because I know he was just joking."

Haynes got up immediately. "Objection, Your Honor. The witness cannot divine another person's state of mind."

"Objection sustained," Justice Dan Jappan ruled. "The jury will disregard the witness's last statement."

"I'm sorry, Your Honor. But surely the witness can speak about his own state of mind." Then Looku turned to Mohabir. "Did YOU feel that Mr. Prashad was serious when he told you that it looked like you took a second wife?"

"No! I did not think that he was serious, because..."

"Objection, Your Honor. This question was asked and answered," Haynes told the judge.

"Objection sustained," Justice Dan Jappan ruled.

"Were there any other customers in Mr. Prashad's shop when he told you that it looked as if you've taken a second wife when he saw you with Mrs. Singh?"

"No, there was no other people there except Mr. Prashad, myself and Phulmattie."

"I have no more questions for this witness."

Mohabir was still scratching his head as he walked out of the witness box.

"Mr. Haynes, do you have any more witnesses?"

"Yes, Your Honor. I would like to call Mr. Sugrim Singh to the stand."

Slippery Ochro walked slowly, but confidently to the stand, obviously enjoying the fact that he was in the limelight. He had many minor cases before, and had witnessed many others, but this was the culmination of all his efforts, and was determined to give this his best shot, especially bearing in mind all the money he stood to get if he won the case. Meanwhile, Mohabir looked at Prashad, who was sitting on the other side of the courtroom, and was looking straight ahead, obviously avoiding eye contact with him. As he raised his hand to scratch his head, Mohabir noticed the blood under his fingernails, and restrained himself. Then he focused his attention on Slippery Ochro who had just finished swearing in.

"Mr. Singh, on the evening January 14, 1966, did your wife tell you that Mr. Prashad told Mr. Mohabir that it looked as if he took a second wife when he saw him with your wife?"

"Yes sir, she did."

"And how did that make you feel?"

"I couldn't sleep at nights, because I was thinking about the whole of Canal talking about Mohabir taking my wife as his second wife."

"Did what Mr. Prashad say affect you in any other way?"

"Yes. It bothered me so much that when I tried to have sex with my wife, I couldn't, because I was thinking about what Prashad said. And I was thinking about the whole of Canal talking about my wife and Mohabir."

"Is it still bothering you today?"

"Yes sir. Even now, I can't have sex with my wife because of what Prashad said. Every time I try to have sex with her, I remember that Prashad tell Mohabir that it look as if he take my wife as his second wife, and I go soft."

Haynes looked at the jury, and saw many men past their prime nodding their heads. Two older women also had sad looks on their faces, and Haynes could only imagine what was going through their minds. "I have no more questions for this witness," he told the judge, as he returned to his seat.

"You may cross-question the witness, Mr. Looku," Justice Dan Jappan told Looku, who got up from his chair, apparently eager to cross-question Slippery Ochro.

"And how are you today, Mr. Singh?" Looku asked Slippery Ochro in a friendly tone.

Slippery Ochro, who had expected a rigorous line of questioning, was taken aback by Looku's smooth manner. "Okay," he answered tentatively.

"You said that you were very bothered by what Mr. Prashad said to Mr. Mohabir about your wife. Is that right?"

"Yes sir. Canal is a small village, and people talk about other people."

"Canal is a small village and people talk about other people. Mr. Singh, did it not bother you that people would talk when you allowed your wife to accompany Mr. Mohabir on a dark night to buy rum?"

Slippery Ochro was silent for a while. Haynes had prepared him for this question, but he forgot what Haynes advised him to say. "We were drinking, and the rum finish. And Mohabir drank too much. We afraid that he might fall down."

"You were afraid that he might fall down. So, you allowed your wife to accompany a man, who was intoxicated, to buy rum on a dark night. And you did this in a village where you told me that people like to talk about other people."

Slippery Ochro was at a loss for words but was rescued by Haynes. "Objection, Your Honor, is Mr. Looku making a statement, or asking a question?"

"Objection sustained," Justice Dan Jappan said. "Mr. Looku, do you have any more questions for the witness?"

"I'm sorry, Your Honor. I have just one or two more questions. Mr. Singh, you said that Mr. Prashad's statement affected sexual relations with your wife. Is that correct?"

Slippery Ochro brightened. "Yes. Ever since Prashad tell Mohabir that it looked as if he took my wife as his second wife, every time I try to have sex with my wife, and I remember what Prashad said, I can't have sex."

"So, what Mr. Prashad said to Mr. Mohabir caused you to be unable to have sex with your wife?"

"Yes, because I imagine what people in Canal were saying about my wife and Mohabir."

"Were you having problems with sex before Prashad said what he did?"

"Not at all. I was able to have sex with my wife every night."

"That's remarkable for a man your age," Looku observed.

Slippery Ochro stood straighter and looked at the jury with pride.

"I have no more questions for this witness," Looku announced.

"Would you like to call any more witnesses, Mr. Haynes?" Justice Dan Jappan asked.

"No, Your Honor."

"Mr. Looku, does the defense have any witnesses it would like to present to the court?" Justice Dan Jappan asked.

"Yes, Your Honor, I'd like to call Mr. Rohit Prashad to the stand."

After Mr. Prashad was sworn in and took the witness stand, Mr. Looku approached him. "Mr. Prashad, did you tell Mr. Mohabir that it looked as if he took a second wife on the evening of the January 14, 1966?"

"Yes, I did, but I was just joking."

"Were there any other customers in your shop when you made this joke with Mr. Mohabir?"

"No, sir. If there were any other customers, I would not have made the joke."

"Was this the only joke you made with Mr. Mohabir?"

"No sir. We always joking with each other. One time, Mohabir told me that he hear that when I was born I was so ugly that the doctor slapped my mother instead of my bum."

The entire courtroom erupted with laughter.

"I have no more questions for this witness," Looku said.

"Mr. Haynes, do you have any questions for the witness?" Justice Dan Jappan asked.

"Just a few, Your Honor," Haynes replied, as he approached the witness stand. "Mr. Prashad, you said that you were just joking when you told Mr. Mohabir that it looked as if he took a second wife when you saw Mrs. Singh with Mr. Mohabir. Am I correct?"

"Yes, I was just joking—"

"A simple 'Yes' or 'No' would be enough," cautioned Haynes. "Did you think of the harm it would do to Mr. and Mrs. Singh's reputations when you made those remarks?"

"I was just joking," Prashad repeated. "Besides, there was nobody else in the store."

Instinctively Haynes realized that he should not have asked that question and told the judge, "No more questions for this witness."

Justice Dan Jappan asked Mr. Looku, "Mr. Looku, do you have any more witnesses?"

"I'd like to call Mr. Cyril Saran to the stand."

Cyril Saran, a slim tall man, dressed in a well pressed black serge suit and an immaculate white shirt, and wearing tinted glasses, walked to the witness stand.

Looku approached the witness stand. "Mr. Saran, please state your name and profession."

"I am a licensed dispenser, and I own a drug store in Good Intent Village."

"And do you know Mr. Sugrim Singh?"

"Yes sir. I do."

"How long have you known Mr. Singh?"

"About five years."

Looku looked at the jury for a few moments before he turned to Cyril Saran. "And how did you know Mr. Singh?"

"He came into my dispensary about five years ago."

Looku looked Cyril Saran straight in the eye. "And why did he come to your dispensary?"

Cyril Saran took great pride in keeping his consultations with everybody who visited his dispensary, secret. Even when his wife, who was an incurable gossip, asked him why certain ladies visited him, he did not betray their confidence. When one of the people working for Looku approached him, Cyril Saran was reluctant to betray Slippery Ochro's confidence, but he remembered that Slippery Ochro was spreading word in Good Intent Village that he was a quack, and a number of frequent customers had stopped coming to his drug store. This was a chance to get back at Slippery Ochro. *Besides*, he thought, *I am not a doctor, and I am not bound by doctor-patient confidentiality*.

"Slippery Ochro asked me whether I had anything to help him have sex with his wife," Cyril Saran replied, avoiding eye contact with Slippery Ochro.

Looku paused for effect and looked at Slippery Ochro and then the jury. "And did you give him any medication?" he asked Cyril Saran.

"Yes. I gave him some tablets, and told him that it would help him."

"What tablets did you give him?"

"I gave him a bottle of Adderall."

"Did you see him after you prescribed Adderall?"

"Yes, he came back about three weeks later, and said that the Adderall did not work."

"Thank you!" Looku told Cyril Saran. "I have no further questions for this witness."

Mr. Haynes declined an opportunity to cross examine Cyril Saran and it was time for the lawyers to present their closing arguments to the jury.

Haynes went first. "Ladies and gentlemen of the jury," he said with a flourish, "we live in a society in which the law is a great equalizer. No matter how much money you have, or how poor you are, you are equal in the eyes of the law. Furthermore, we live in a society where the strong cannot take advantage of the weak. This includes the physically strong, or the financially strong. A blow from a hand can hurt you, but words can hurt you more sometimes." He turned to face the jury. "A physical injury can heal. But the hurt that words cause can last a lifetime."

Haynes turned dramatically to Prashad. "Mr. Prashad is a prominent owner of a grocery store and a rum shop, in a small village where everybody knows everybody's business. He said that he was making a joke when he said that it looked as if Mohabir took Phulmattie, a very chaste and upright woman, as his second wife. How would everybody in Canal know that he was joking? Had Mohabir gone to his shop with the Pandit's wife would he have said that? Or did he feel that he could say anything about Mr. Singh's wife because he is poor? Even if Mr. Prashad meant what he said as a joke, what effect did that have on Mr. Singh?" Then he looked at an elderly juror. "How would you feel if somebody tells another man that it looked as if he took your wife as his second wife?" The juror at whom Haynes was looking squirmed, and Haynes took pity on him, and looked away.

"I know that you will find Mr. Prashad liable for the hurt and humiliation he has caused Mr. Singh, a poor, but proud man, who has lent a helping hand to many of his villagers."

Haynes looked at Slippery Ochro with something like pride as he made his way to his seat. It was Looku's turn to address the jury.

Looku stood up, and looked at Slippery Ochro and Phulmattie, before going to the jury box. "Ladies and gentlemen," he said, "Mr. Haynes has made some worthwhile points, but what he lacked was the context." Looku looked at Haynes, who had a puzzled look on his face. "Mr. Singh, a poor, but proud man, as Mr. Haynes described him, asked Mr. Mohabir's permission to build a small house on his land, and Mr. Mohabir kindly granted him permission. They were drinking on the night in question, and Mr. Singh's wife, a pure and chaste woman, according to Mr. Haynes, decided to accompany Mr. Mohabir to the shop on a dark night to buy, not a pound of sugar, not two pounds of potatoes, but a bottle of rum.

"We heard from Mr. Mohabir how he and Mr. Prashad were always joking and making fun of each other. And we heard from Mr. Sugrim Singh how he was negatively affected by the publicity that Mr. Prashad told Mr. Mohabir that it looked as if he took a second wife. We also heard from Mr. Prashad that there was nobody else present at the shop when he told Mohabir that it looked as if he took a second wife when he and Phulmattie went to buy a bottle of rum.

"How, then, did the whole of Canal No. 2 know that Mr. Prashad told Mr. Mohabir that it looked as if he took a second wife when he saw him with Mr. Singh's wife? Who was responsible for the publicity? Mr. Singh saw an opportunity to get some money from Mr. Prashad and seized it. In an effort to garner sympathy from members of the jury, Mr. Singh complained that the problems caused by the rumors spread when Mr. Prashad told Mr. Mohabir that it looked as if he took a second wife when he saw him with Mrs. Singh caused him to be unable to have sex with his wife. We learned from Mr. Cyril Saran that Mr. Singh was having problems performing sexually long before that. And to emphasize, he was the one who started the rumors, because he wanted to benefit financially from them."

Justice Dan Jappan then asked the jury to consider the evidence in their deliberations and come to a decision. "Court will be reconvened on December 17, by which time the jury should have reached a verdict." Justice Dan Jappan banged his gavel and stood up.

**

Mohabir found himself in Polo's hire car along with Prashad on the return trip to Canal.

Prashad retained a sullen silence, while Mohabir was anxiously waiting for an excuse to talk to him.

Polo broke the uncomfortable silence. "What happen with court case?" he asked Prashad.

"The jury gon decide. We go back to court on December seventeen."

This gave Mohabir the opportunity for which he had been waiting. "I tell the judge and jury that Prashad been only joking when he tell me that it look like I take a second wife," he told all the passengers in the car.

"And Slippery Ochro use that as an excuse to take me to court," Prashad countered. Then he looked Mohabir in his eyes, and observed. "You and Dularie think you so kind, and you allow Slippery and Phulmattie to build their house on you land. But them people smarter than you and Dularie any day."

Apparently, Prashad wanted to say this for quite a while, because after he said it, he was visibly relaxed, and breathed a sigh of relief.

"They smarter than most of we in this car," Polo remarked. "They don't work, so they use all their time to think how to smart out people."

None of the passengers disputed this statement. Bangra, who sat in the back seat, expostulated further. "Any one of them can outsmart anybody in this car. When you put Slippery Ochro and Phulmattie together, nobody can beat them."

Mohabir wanted to ask Prashad whether they could have a drink at his shop, but hesitated. Besides, he was anxious to go home and inform Dularie of the day's proceedings.

As soon as he crossed the bridge spanning the four-foot drainage trench, she walked quickly up to him. "Wha' happen? Prashad win the case?"

"The jury got to decide," Mohabir told her. "Prashad and Slippery Ochro got to go back to court on December seventeen to find out who win." Then he thought for a while as they walked to the bottom house. "I don't got to go, but I want to go to find out what happen with the case."

"Oh! You become like Slippery Ochro and Phulmattie now. You like court case." Dularie immediately regretted saying this, as Mohabir's hand started scratching his head. "But I know that you want to find out if yuh friend win or lose this case," she told him, as she held his hand.

**

Slippery Ochro and Phulmattie avoided Mohabir and his wife, as they all anxiously waited for December 17. Both families avoided prolonged eye contact when they had brief glimpses of each other between the coffee trees. When decision day arrived, Slippery Ochro and Phulmattie, and Mohabir took separate cars. Mohabir did not even see Prashad when he joined Polo's car to get the 7:30 ferry. But he did see Haynes with Slippery Ochro and Phulmattie, and Looku with Prashad on the verandah of the Victoria Law Courts. He did not join any of the groups, but when the case was called, he chose to sit behind Prashad and Looku, and ignored the stares of Slippery Ochro and Phulmattie.

Justice Dan Jappan formally entered the courtroom, and the court orderly announced in a loud voice, "Court is now in session."

After Justice Dan Jappan sat down with a flourish, he asked the foreman of the jury, "Has the jury reached a verdict?"

"Yes, Your Honor. The jury finds that the defendant, Mr. Prashad, not liable for any damages, and that the plaintiff, Mr. Sugrim Singh, should be liable for Mr. Prashad's court costs, including legal fees."

Prashad smiled widely, and reached to shake Looku's hand. On the other side of the courtroom, Slippery Ochro was shooting daggers with his looks alternatively at Prashad and at Mohabir, who he felt did not give strong enough evidence.

"The court dismisses the lawsuit against Mr. Prashad, and orders Mr. Sugrim Singh to pay legal costs, to be determined, to Mr. Prashad." Justice Dan Jappan smacked his gavel on the table, stood up and left the court room for his chambers, leaving Slippery Ochro still staring maliciously at Prashad and Mohabir, with occasional glances at Looku.

The case was finished in time for everybody to get the three o'clock ferry. However, when Slippery Ochro saw Mohabir and Prashad line up to buy tickets for the ferry, he decided to wait until the next ferry and he diverted into Stabroek Market.

"I glad that the judge ruled in your favor," Mohabir told Prashad, as they waited in the line.

Prashad had vowed never to speak to Mohabir again, but he was heartened by the ruling, and relented. "Me too! I make one innocent joke, and look how much time and money it cost me."

"The judge ruled that Slippery Ochro got to pay your legal fees. And I did give evidence that you been only joking."

"Where he gon get the money from? He isn't working. He don't have any property. You gon give him the money to pay me?"

Mohabir did not have time to answer, because they had arrived at the ticket counter. In the ferry, they were relieved that Slippery Ochro was nowhere in sight. They had seen him enter Stabroek Market, but were unsure whether he would come out in time to catch the ferry. They spoke very little to each other, but both felt that there was a spark of hope that their friendship would be rekindled. When they walked out together from the ferry at Vreedenhoop, they were greeted by Polo.

"What happen with the court case?" Polo asked.

"The judge dismiss the case," Prashad said, knowing full well that the news would be relayed to the whole of Canal before long.

Mohabir decided to give some additional information. "And the judge award court costs to Prashad."

"You won't see any money from Slippery Ochro," Polo told Prashad, putting his right hand to his face, and his index finger under one eye and the middle finger under the other, and pulling the skin down.

When they approached Mohabir's house, Polo slowed down to drop him off at Gobin's bridge.

Prashad told him, "Don't stop here. Let we go to my shop, and I gon put a bottle of rum on the table."

Mohabir, glad to be on Prashad's good side once more, breathed a sigh of relief. By then, they were the only passengers in the car, and Polo pulled over at the side of the road and the three went into Prashad's rum shop.

Prashad's wife, Indra, immediately asked him, "What happen to the court case?"

"It dismiss," Prashad said. "And Slippery Ochro got to pay court costs."

"The judge don't know Slippery Ochro?" Indra asked. "He gon give Slippery Ochro the money to pay you court costs?"

"At least Slippery Ochro will not get a red cent from me," Prashad consoled his wife. "He think that he can become rich off my sweat." Then he turned to Mohabir. "Slippery Ochro gon still live on your land?"

"I don't know how to get rid of him. How can I evict him? I am tired of courts."

"I got a plan," Prashad told Mohabir. "I gon tell you later."

The three drank until late in the night, and by the time Mohabir went home, Dularie was fast asleep. When Mohabir went to the kitchen to eat something before going to bed, he saw a note from Dularie on the kitchen table. It said, *I glad that Prashad win the case. I hear that you drinking with Prashad at his place. I glad. The people mouth in Canal can really run.*

Mohabir thought. *Dularie know about the case before I come home. I should'a come home and tell sheer before I go drinking with Prashad and Polo.*

Chapter 15

"Seek freedom and become captive of your desires. Seek discipline and find your liberty."
—Frank Herbert—

The following morning, Mohabir and Dularie were sitting on their verandah when they saw Slippery Ochro and Phulmattie walking towards Gobin Bridge to get a hire car. They did not see the couple until three days later when they saw them walking home at about 8 a.m. Mohabir and Dularie were having lunch when they heard a knocking at front door at about 12:00 noon on the same day. When Mohabir opened it, he saw Dugdug.

"So Slippery Ochro move out?" Dugdug asked him.

"What do you mean?"

"He and his wife get a car at about ten-thirty this morning. I see them carrying two big suitcases and some small bags. When I ask them what was happening, Slippery Ochro say that he going to his cousin in Wakenaam. He say to tell Prashad that if he want any money from him, to go and see him in Wakenaam. He say to tell Prashad that his cousin know some bad people in Wakenaam, and that they gon like to meet him."

"Leh we go and see if he house empty," Dularie told Mohabir and Dugdug.

The three walked through the coffee trees to Slippery Ochro's house. Sure enough, the front door was open, and when they walked in, the house was empty except for some old clothes on the floor, and a straw hat hanging on a nail on the wall.

Mohabir said, "Prashad na gon get his money, but we get rid of Slippery Ochro. I gon burn this house rass down. It remind me too much of Slippery Ochro."

Dularie was surprised to hear her husband swear, but Dugdug replied encouragingly, as he looked at the thatched roof, "The grass roof gon burn nice. Me and Snakeskin gon do it."

"Make sure that the trees around the house don't get burn," Dularie cautioned.

Mohabir turned to Dugdug. "It too early to drink.But tell Snakeskin to come to Prashad this afternoon. I gon buy you boys a drink."

Mohabir and Dularie spent the remainder of the day laughing and enjoying the fact that Slippery Ochro and Phulmattie were no longer around to intrude in their lives.

"You better eat before you go drinking with Snakeskin and Dugdug," Dularie cautioned her husband. "Or else you gon get drunk, and can't eat when you come home."

"Leh we take one before we eat," Mohabir told his wife. "Leh we celebrate we freedom from Slippery Ochro and Phulmattie." He felt so elated that he was tempted to tell his wife about his escapade with Phulmattie, but thought better of it, as he poured large drinks for himself and Dularie.

After dinner, Mohabir went to Prashad, where they saw Dugdug and Snakeskin sitting at a table, and drinking from a quarter bottle of rum. He immediately went to the counter and bought a large bottle of Russian Bear and four bottles of Coke, and joined them. A few minutes later, they were joined by an ecstatic Prashad, who was too relieved by the dismissal of the court case to worry about the money he would not get from Slippery Ochro.

After the first drink, Mohabir felt obliged to remind Prashad, "I told you that I gon say that you been only joking."

"I stop joking," Prashad replied. "Joking cost too much money." And he laughed as he looked at Mohabir, Snakeskin and Dugdug.

"As long as Dugdug and me live in Canal, nobody can touch the two of you," Snakeskin told Mohabir and Prashad.

It was about one in the morning when they left Prashad's rum shop, and Mohabir staggered home. He slept with his clothes on, and he and Dularie were sound asleep when they heard the crackling of flames at about four o'clock in the morning. They were worried that there was a fire in their house, and hurried to check, but realized that the crackling was outside their house, and opened a window to check. They had to shield their eyes as they saw a huge fire, and after the initial shock, both realized that Dugdug and Snakeskin kept their promise. They decided to leave the fire experts to do their job, and went back to bed.

Both Mohabir and Dularie felt a heavy weight lift from their shoulders, but Mohabir was the more relieved of the two. He was still feeling the effects of the alcohol he had drunk, but he could not help thinking, as he spooned Dularie, *I wonder who from Wakenaam Slippery Ochro taking to court, and who Phulmattie climbing on top of.*

THE END

ABOUT THE AUTHOR

Ken Ramphal was born in Canal No. 2 Polder in Guyana. He was a teacher before he joined the Guyana Defense Force as an officer cadet, and rose to the rank of captain. Ken was the ADC to the acting Governor General, Sir Edward Luckhoo and the President, His Excellency Arthur Chung, before he immigrated to Canada in 1975. Ken holds a B.A from the University of Guyana and a Ph.D from the University of Toronto. He was a teacher, an anti-racist Consultant in the East York Board of Education, and an Education Officer in the Ontario Ministry of Education. He is currently retired, and is the author of six books, including one, which he co-wrote with his sister and brother. He has also published a number of articles in educational journals. His book *Slippery Ochro* won 3rd prize at the Guyana Prize For Literature (fiction) 2023.

ALSO FROM MIDDLEROAD PUBLISHERS

MiddleRoad | Publishers

www.middleroadpublishers.ca

Making Literature See The Light Of Day

ALL BOOKS AVAILABLE AT AMAZON WORLDWIDE.
eBook versions available from all eBook channels

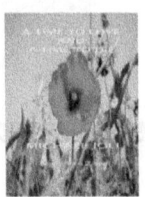

A TIME TO LOVE AND A TIME TO DIE

By Michael Joll

Finely drawn characters. Visually dramatic, tense and emotionally satisfying, this is one of the finest novels of the Great War. In this poignant story, the writing stands in stark contrast with the unvarnished brutality of trench warfare.

ATTITUDE

By Dave Moores

Fresh, gritty and laced with dry humour, Attitude is a fast-paced story readers of all ages won't want to put down. It's dead of winter and an outbreak of weird stuff, random acts of vandalism are unsettling the citizens of Southmead.

DANCING MY WAY TO 80

By Doris Naraine

Biography published privately and not available for sale.

DOWN INDEPENDENCE BOULEVARD AND OTHER STORIES

by Ken Puddicombe

"A brilliant collection of stories telling the tales of people forced to leave their homes...craving the past, escaping from racial conflicts and dictatorship..."—Judith Kopacsi Gelberger, author of *Heroes Don't Cry*.

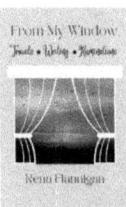

FROM MY WINDOW

By Rena Flannigan

Memories of travels, all come alive as Rena transports us to another time...her words paint the picture and we see through her eyes.

- 178 -

GABRIELLE

By Michael Joll

Gabrielle transcends time and space, taking the reader on a journey to Poland, France, Holland and Israel as she searches for her identity.

I WENT TO THE END OF THE RAINBOW

by Pramita Chakraborty

A beautifully illustrated, captivating tale about a young child who can't sleep and embarks on a adventure through the colours of the rainbow.

GENERATIONS

Biography published privately and not available for sale.

JUNTA

By Ken Puddicombe

"A gripping story (of) an imperfect democracy…the tension…builds increasingly from page to page." — Rico Downer, author of *There Once Was a Little England*

HACKER

by MICHAEL JOLL

Teenage hacker Penny McBride joins detective Sgt. Richard Williams to solve her father's murder and they both come up against the Mob.

LOVE HAS TWO MOONS

"The garden which my wife has created, it is as much a work of art as a painting by a master spirit or a piece of perfect music by a composer."—Ian Mc Donald, author, poet.

RACING WITH THE RAIN

By Ken Puddicombe

"Puddicombe's brilliant novel...an historic political conflict in Guyana, during the Cold War and the cold cynicism and tragic irony of a state sacrificed to super-power hegemony." -Frank Birbalsingh, author of *Novels and The Nation: Essays in Canadian*

RUTHLESS RHYTHMS

By Judith Gelberger

If poetry is a window into the soul of the author, Judith Gelberger has opened one which illuminates some of the most painful emotions and experiences of human existence...—Raymond Holmes – Author of *Witnesses And Other Short Stories*

SCALING NEW HEIGHTS

Anthology

Forty-two pieces from the members of Pakaraima Writers Group are featured in this their first collection of poetry and non-fiction travel articles

SNAPSHOTS OF OUR LIVES

Anthology

Authors Ram Jagessar (Trinidad), Roop Misir and Kennard Ramphal (Guyana) combined their talents to produce a fifty-one-piece Collection of stirring anecdotes. These stories traverse *THE HOMELAND*, set in Trinidad and Guyana, and *THE IMMIGRANT EXPERIENCE* in Canada where they migrated as young men.

SPARKLES AND KARIM

By Dave Moores

Major Michelle Wilson, callsign *Sparkles*, a US fighter pilot, and Karim Hamid, callsign *Black Flag*, a US soldier of Iraqi descent, come up against ISIS in a perilous mission in Iraq.

TASTE MY WORDS

By Lisa Freemantle

Freemantle's compositions are imbued with a highly poetic energy instilling in the reader a subtle, penetrating fever of contentment...." —Dr. Franklin Mohan, author *Love Has Two Moons and Other Stories*

THE GARDEN

By Ian McDonald

Ian McDonald's poems are full of light and love. His easy style about the beauty of nature connects with his readers.

TOWARDS THE PEBBLED SHORE

By Peter Jailall

"...thoughtfully conceived, expressed movingly and written with great clarity. I think this may be Peter's best book yet. It lifts the heart."

Ian McDonald, author The Garden and other works

TROPICAL SCENES

By Ken Puddicombe

Each poem covers more ground than lengthy chapters.

A pungent cocktail of choppy romance, corporate larceny and the thrills and spills of sailboat racing, Windward Legs is the rousing and captivating story of a woman's journey to rediscover who she is.

UNFATHOMABLE AND OTHER POEMS

by Ken Puddicombe

These poems cover a variety of themes, all connected to a childhood growing up in British Guiana, the rise of nationalism and the pre- and post-independence eras.

WITNESSES AND OTHER STORIES

By Raymond Holmes

"Suspenseful, historical, futuristic and riveting...stories and characters who will stay with you." —Bruce A. Hanson, Award winning author of adult and children's fiction.

WEALTH THROUGH REAL ESTATE INVESTING

By Jay Brijpaul

Jay Brijpaul has tapped his vast experience and expertise in the Real Estate industry. This book provides comprehensive coverage of What, How, When, Where to invest in real estate.

WINDWARD LEGS

By Dave Moores